GREAT LIVES OBSERVED

Gerald Emanuel Stearn, *General Editor*

EACH VOLUME IN THE SERIES VIEWS THE CHARACTER AND
ACHIEVEMENT OF A GREAT WORLD FIGURE IN THREE PER-
SPECTIVES—THROUGH HIS OWN WORDS, THROUGH THE OPIN-
IONS OF HIS CONTEMPORARIES, AND THROUGH RETROSPECTIVE
JUDGMENTS—THUS COMBINING THE INTIMACY OF AUTOBIOG-
RAPHY, THE IMMEDIACY OF EYEWITNESS OBSERVATION, AND
THE OBJECTIVITY OF MODERN SCHOLARSHIP.

JOHN C. RULE, editor of this volume in the Great Lives Observed series, is Professor of History at The Ohio State University. His articles have appeared in numerous journals, among
them *French Historical Studies, The William and Mary Quarterly, History and Theory,* and the *American Quarterly.* His
most recent essays have been published in *William III and
Louis XIV* and *Essays in Diplomatic History.* He is editor of
and contributor to *The Early Modern Era 1648–1770* and *Louis
XIV and the Craft of Kingship.*

GREAT LIVES OBSERVED

LOUIS XIV

Edited by JOHN C. RULE

*When one has the State in
view, one is working for
oneself. The good of the
one makes the glory of the
other.*

Louis XIV

A SPECTRUM BOOK

PRENTICE-HALL, INC., ENGLEWOOD CLIFFS, N.J.

Library of Congress Cataloging in Publication Data

RULE, JOHN C comp.
   Louis XIV

   (Great lives observed) (A Spectrum Book)
   Bibliography: p.
   1. Louis XIV, King of France, 1638–1715.
DC129.R8   944'.033'0924 [B]   73–16430
ISBN 0–13–540773–7
ISBN 0–13–540765–6 (pbk.)

© 1974 by PRENTICE-HALL, INC.,
Englewood Cliffs, N.J.

A SPECTRUM BOOK

PRENTICE-HALL INTERNATIONAL, INC. (*London*)
PRENTICE-HALL OF AUSTRALIA PTY., LTD. (*Sydney*)
PRENTICE-HALL OF CANADA, LTD. (*Toronto*)
PRENTICE-HALL OF INDIA PRIVATE LIMITED (*New Delhi*)
PRENTICE-HALL OF JAPAN, INC. (*Tokyo*)

714314

Contents

v

To my Mother

Introduction

Born on September 5, 1638, amidst the general rejoicing of the Court and country, Louis XIV became king of France on May 16, 1643. Two days after his accession, the young king and his mother, Anne of Austria, rode in state to the Parlement of Paris, where the magistrates declared Anne sole regent. The queen mother nominated Jules, Cardinal Mazarin, to the post of principal minister, and, together with an able group of advisers, Anne and Mazarin ruled France until 1661.

France in the seventeenth century was the most populous and probably the wealthiest country in Western Europe, yet it was beset by problems that Anne and Mazarin could not solve. Taxes soared, inflation absorbed profits, periodic provincial revolts devastated the countryside. The middle class feared declining revenue from their bonds and lands, and the magistrates became increasingly zealous in defending their prerogatives. These perennial problems were exacerbated by the need for France to maintain large armies in the Low Countries and the Germanies to fight in the Thirty Years' War (1618–48), which continued as a Franco-Spanish conflict until 1659. Mazarin's attempts to raise additional revenues were resisted by the upper middle class, the magistrates, and the greater nobility. In the summer of 1648 their complaints culminated in collective protests clamoring for Mazarin's removal. Anne of Austria, a proud and imperious woman, dismissed the outcries and had several of the leading protesters, including members of the Parlement of Paris, arrested. The sparks of rebellion ignited a conflagration known as the *Frondes* (civil wars), extinguished only in 1653.

Louis XIV thus grew up in an atmosphere of political unrest and among men who were either open or potential enemies of his mother and Mazarin. Fear, mistrust, and mendacity left their marks on the young king; during the rest of his life he confided in very few people, and he viewed with suspicion his "over-mighty subjects," especially princes of the royal blood—who might pose a threat to his family—and quarrelsome churchmen and dis-

1

senters in religion or politics—who might question his authority
(see his *Mémoires*, pp. 12 ff.).

Yet despite the troubled times, Louis's formal education was
not neglected as several of his biographers, particularly the Duke
of Saint-Simon, claimed. The young king received adequate training in foreign languages—certainly he understood Italian and
Spanish, although his Latin remained poor; he read and enjoyed
history and geography; and he loved music and the theater. He
spoke well but knew how to keep his own counsel. His political
ideas were most certainly molded by the times: his natural bent
toward pragmatism was reinforced, as were his caution, his belief
in the power of the crown, and his willingness to listen to and to
weigh advice (see Lavisse and Rule).

Forgoing his personal wishes, Louis married in 1660 Maria-
Theresa, eldest daughter of Philip IV and niece to Anne of Austria. Petite and blond, Maria proved to be a devoted if dull wife.
She brought with her a dowry of 500,000 crowns, agreed to at the
Franco-Spanish peace signed at the Pyrenees in 1659. It was this
dowry, however, that was to cause controversy in the future. Few
of the French ministers, or the Spanish for that matter, thought
it would ever be paid; and there was a clause in the treaty stating
that if it were not paid, the Spanish Succession, failing a male
heir in Spain, would revert to Maria, as the elder daughter of
the house, and to her children.

A year after the marriage alliance with Spain, Louis was faced
with a major constitutional crisis at home. Mazarin died on
March 9, 1661. The king's courtiers at once approached him to
find out who would be the new prime minister. Louis's surprising
reply was that they should report to him personally. If the king's
advisers had doubts as to his determination to be his own chief
minister, these were soon dispelled. Louis meant to rule; indeed
he had been urged to take the reins of government by Mazarin
himself, and for the next fifty-four years he kept his promise
(see Lavisse, Chapter 9).

The early years of Louis's personal reign were filled with
tumult, change, and promise. To meet the challenges of the time
Louis began at once to reform his councils (see Chapter 13),
selecting as his closest advisers three men who had served
Mazarin: Jean-Baptiste Colbert, Michel Le Tellier, and Hugues
de Lionne. History has honored Colbert and largely neglected

Le Tellier and Lionne. Yet Michel Le Tellier had a great hand in reforming the army and in sending out commissioners-on-mission (called *intendants*) to enforce the law in the provinces. His son, François-Michel Le Tellier, the Marquis de Louvois, continued his father's work, becoming Louis's greatest war minister. Lionne also left his mark as an able diplomatist and a dedicated administrator. Together they were known as the *Triade*, or "great trio." Colbert, however, still—and perhaps rightly—attracts our attention because through him Louis initiated popular and comprehensive reforms of the laws, which began with a codification of the civil codes in 1667, criminal codes in 1670, a new commercial code in 1673, and further revisions under Chancellor Pontchartrain at the end of the reign. In the economic–commercial sphere Louis and Colbert encouraged the founding of new trading companies, of a vastly increased merchant marine, of the manufacture of luxury goods, and of vast schemes for public works, of which the construction of royal palaces was but one phase. Louis and Colbert also undertook a reformation of the cultural life of the kingdom by establishing royal academies for the support of scholarly and artistic work, the most famous being the Academy of Sciences (1666). The impetus that Colbert gave to these reforms lived long after his death in 1683.

The rise to power of the Colberts and the other ministerial families represented the triumph in seventeenth-century France of the "men of the pen," the greater civil servants, who in many instances were themselves nobles of the robe or who had been ennobled. These bureaucrats or civil servants tended not to make a clean break with the past but, rather, to further the king's plans through established institutions like the Council of State (Chapter 13), the parlements, the local estates, and the provincial governors. Although royal agents such as provincial and army *intendants* were sent to coordinate the efforts of the local magistracy, they tended to work closely with entrenched local interests rather than suppress or circumvent them.

Louis XIV listened to his ministers but often followed his own inclinations. For instance, it was his desire—flying in the face of Colbert's wishes—to build the palace of Versailles and abandon his permanent residence in Paris. Louis despised Paris: it reminded him of rebellion and of his tutelage. Also, as the king grew older the court increased in size to nearly fifteen thousand courtiers and servants; it needed a new setting, which Louis found thirteen miles southwest of Paris in the hilly country around his father's château of Versailles. By 1682, not only the court but also the ministers and the bureaucracy had moved to Versailles, not to return to Paris until the October Days of 1789.

Louis, ably supported by Colbert and his family and by the Le Telliers and their family, interested himself not only in domestic reform but also in international relations. As Louis tells us in his *Mémoires,* France emerged from the Thirty Years' War and the conflict with Spain stronger than any other European nation. In order to underscore this point, Louis opted for an aggressive foreign policy designed to remind his neighbors of the grandeur and power of France. In 1662, Charles II of England, under pressure from Louis's government, sold the important port of Dunkirk to France and in 1670 allied himself to the French by the Secret Treaty of Dover. Philip IV bowed to his son-in-law's wishes by recognizing that French ambassadors had right of precedence over his own. Sweden, Brandenburg, Poland, and many German and Italian princes sought subsidies from Louis XIV, and the Ottoman Empire made advantageous trade agreements with the French. Three major powers in the early years challenged Louis's bid for European hegemony: the Dutch Netherlands, the Emperor Leopold I, and the Pope.

In the years between the 1660's and the 1690's Louis moved against all three of his opponents. The Dutch were Louis's most hated foes. They represented a combined commercial–diplomatic threat to France: their vast commercial fleet served as the major carriers of world goods; their colonial empire flourished; and their interest in the Spanish Netherlands (Belgium) proved a curb to Louis XIV's ambitions in that area. Dutch defenses were put to the test when, in 1672, French armies, in a dramatic crossing of the Rhine, invaded the Netherlands, causing panic in the major Dutch cities and the fall of the Dutch government. The young *stadtholder* (military leader of five of the seven provinces) William of Orange (later William III) upheld the honor of his house and of his country by raising an army at home and a coalition of powers abroad. Although successful in repulsing the French invasion of the Netherlands, William and the Emperor Leopold I could not prevent Louis from seizing (for the second time) the Free County of Burgundy (the Franche-Comté) and a number of border fortresses along the northern and northeastern frontiers. At the Dutch town of Nijmegen (in 1677–79) a compromise peace settlement was made in which the French retained the Free County and a number of the border fortresses, while conceding an advantageous economic treaty to the Dutch. Some historians, particularly in the early twentieth century, viewed the years 1679–81 as the apogee of Louis XIV's reign (Chapter 9).

The second of Louis's principal challengers, the Papacy, felt Louis's ire even before the Dutch. Popes Innocent X (1644–55), Alexander VII (1655–67), and Innocent XI (1676–89) were opponents of France. Louis, exercising his prerogative as head of the Gallican church, harassed the Holy See in matters both political and ecclesiastical. At a point near the end of Innocent XI's pontificate (1688), the Pope, irritated by France's foreign policy, secretly excommunicated Louis; this after the French king had ostentatiously cleansed the French church (in 1685) of heresy by revoking privileges granted the Protestants in 1598 under the Edict of Nantes. During the reigns of Pope Innocent XII (1691–1700) and Pope Clement XI (1700–21), there was a dramatic shift in policy. Louis made his peace with the Papacy and, indeed, solicited the reigning Pope's support for his domestic policies. Yet we must keep in mind, as statements in his *Mémoires* attest, that Louis always mistrusted churchmen, at home and abroad, and that this mistrust did not abate as he grew older.

In the 1680's, the king directed his diplomatic–military offensive against the traditional enemy of France, the House of Habsburg, whose titular head was Leopold I of Austria, a stubborn opponent, "an obstinate and tenacious guardian of his family's rights, and ultimately Louis's most determined enemy." Louis countered Austrian power on the Rhine and in the Low Countries by annexing the city of Strasbourg (1681); by besieging fortresses in the County of Luxembourg (1682–84); by pressing his sister-in-law's claims in the Palatinate (1685–88); and finally by sending his armies to invade the Rhineland area (1688–89). The emperor met the challenge by supporting a coalition of Louis's opponents, known as the League of Augsburg. The French invasion of the Rhineland sparked a war that engulfed Europe and the colonial empires abroad (the War of the League of Augsburg, 1688–97).

The French people suffered bitterly during this world war:

armies grew greatly in size and so did taxes; a new state subven-
tion, the capitation or head tax, was inaugurated in 1694. In the
same year France was struck by plague, famine, and a severe winter: over a million people died. Louis and his ministers anxiously
sought peace, which was signed only in 1697 at the Congress of
Ryswick. By the Ryswick Treaty Louis managed to retain many
of his border fortresses and Alsace, including Strasbourg.

But Ryswick was only a truce. The question of the Spanish
Succession, which had haunted the councils of Europe since 1659,
demanded an answer. Carlos II of Spain, Louis's brother-in-law,
was close to death. Would the whole of the Spanish inheritance
go to the Austrian Habsburgs? Would it go to Louis and his
children? Would it be divided among the Austrians, the French,
and other European powers, notably the English and Dutch?
Louis and William III chose the last course and twice divided the inheritance through partition treaties (1698 and 1700).
Both efforts at arbitration failed, due largely to the opposition
of the Emperor Leopold and of Carlos II himself. Just before his
death, Carlos left the entire Spanish Inheritance to Louis's
grandson Philip of Anjou and, failing him, to the Emperor's
second son, Charles. Louis, after some debate in his council, accepted Carlos's Will.

Outraged, William, the Dutch, and the emperor called for war,
which came in the summer of 1701. The War of the Spanish Succession (1701–14) was the dreariest of all the conflicts of Louis's
reign, yet the most inevitable. Immense losses of life occurred:
at the battle of Malplaquet (1709), for instance, the Allies lost
24,000 dead and the French 15,000. A pall fell over Louis's court:
Colbert de Torcy, the king's foreign minister, describes Louis's
tantrums and tears, his fear that God had abandoned France (see
pp. 95 ff.). Finally, in 1710–11, the tide of war began to turn in
Louis's favor, and in 1712, after several abortive attempts at
making a peace treaty, the Allies and France met at the Dutch
cathedral town of Utrecht to draw up one of the most famous
peace settlements of modern times, the Treaty of Utrecht, ranking
in importance with the treaties of Westphalia (1648) and Vienna
(1814–15). It marked the end of an era. Out of this conflict
emerged three clearly demarked spheres of influence. The first
was headed by Great Britain, the British Empire, and the client
nations of Portugal, the Dutch Netherlands, Ireland, Hanover

(after 1714), and Denmark. The second coalition consisted of France, the French Empire, the German client states of Bavaria and Cologne, Pope Clement XI, and, after the 1720's, Spain and the Spanish Empire. The third sphere of influence fell to the Austrian Habsburgs as rulers of Bohemia, of the Austrian crown lands, and as suzerains of Hungary and northern Italy. Two potential rivals to Austrian power loomed distantly in 1713–14: the kingdom of Prussia and the empire of Russia. The Utrecht settlement marked the appearance of a worldwide balance of power that was to exist down to 1793–94 and was to be reestablished after 1815 for another generation.

Louis himself, overwhelmed by cares of state, and reaching the advanced age of seventy-five in the year the peace treaties were signed, retreated more often to the calm of Madame de Maintenon's sitting room (Chapter 5), where he listened to chamber music and conferred with his ministers. The auxiliary councils of dispatches, of finances, of conscience, met less often (Chapter 6). One minister, Beauvilliers, died in 1713; another, Chancellor Pontchartrain, retired in 1714. Louis's grandson—the talented Duke of Burgundy—Burgundy's wife, and one of their children died in 1712; another grandson died in 1714. It was a time of perpetual mourning at court. Finally, in the summer of 1714, Louis agreed to draw up a Will (Chapter 3). Prophetically, within the year (September 1, 1715) he was dead, at the age of seventy-seven years less five days.

Chronology of the Life of Louis XIV

1638	(September 5) Birth of Louis.
1640	(September 21) Birth of his brother Philippe.
1642	(December) Death of Cardinal Richelieu.
1643	(May 16) Louis XIII's death.
	(May 19) Battle of Rocroy: France victorious over Spain.
	Anne becomes regent, Mazarin chief minister.
1648	(Fall) Outbreak of the Parlementary Fronde.
	(October 24) Peace of Westphalia.
1649	(January 6) Flight of king to St. Germain-en-Laye.
1650	(January 18) Arrest of the princes (Condé, Conti, Longueville).
	Princely Frondes.
1651	(February 6) Mazarin flees to Germany.
	(September 7) King comes of age.
1652	(October 21) Court and king return to Paris.
1653	(February 3) Return of Mazarin to Paris—end of Frondes.
1654	(June 7) Coronation of the king at Rheims.
1658	(June 14) Battle of the Dunes won by Turenne over the Spanish.
1659	(November 7) Peace of the Pyrenees.
1660	(June 9) Louis marries Maria-Theresa of Spain.
1661	(March 9) Death of Cardinal Mazarin.
	Beginning of Louis's personal reign.
	(September 5) Fouquet arrested.
	Louis XIV begins reforms in his Councils.
1665	(September 16) Death of Philip IV of Spain.
	Colbert appointed Controller-General.
1666	(January 20) Death of Anne of Austria.
1667	(May) War of Devolution.
1668	(January 19) Secret Partition Treaty with the Emperor Leopold I.
	(January 23) First Triple Alliance. (The Dutch, England, and Sweden)
	(May 2) Peace of Aix-la-Chapelle.
1670	(May) Treaty of Dover with Charles II of England.

1672	(May) Invasion of Dutch Netherlands.
1673	(July/August) Coalition of the Hague against France.
1678–79	Treaties of Nijmegen.
1680	(March) Beginning of "Reunions" policy, by which France annexed lands along her north and northeastern borders.
1681	(September 30) France seizes Strasbourg as part of the reunion policy.
1682	(March) Four Gallican Articles of French Church. (August 6) Birth of the Duke of Burgundy. Court and government formally move to Versailles.
1683	(July 30) Death of Maria-Theresa. (September 6) Death of Colbert.
1684	Probable year of the secret marriage to Madame de Maintenon.
1685	(October 18) Revocation of the Edict of Nantes.
1688	Glorious Revolution in England.
1688–89	Beginning of the War of the League of Augsburg (or Nine Years' War).
1689	(August) Fénelon named preceptor to the Duke of Burgundy and Duke of Beauvilliers named his governor.
1691	(July) Death of Louvois. (July) Reorganization of the ministry with the entry to the *Conseil d'en haut* of Pomponne and Beauvilliers.
1694	Great famine in France. Quietism attacked.
1697	(August) Fénelon exiled. (September 30) Treaty of Ryswick, ending the War of the League of Augsburg. (December 6) Marriage of Duke of Burgundy to Maria-Adelaide of Savoy.
1698	(October 11) First Partition Treaty.
1700	(March 13) Second Partition Treaty. (November 1) Death of Carlos II. Philip of Anjou becomes king of Spain as Philip V.
1701	(September 7) Grand Alliance of the Hague against France.
1702	(May 15) Allies declare war on France. War of the Spanish Succession.
1704	(August 13) Defeat of the French at Blenheim.
1705	(May 6) Death of Emperor Leopold I of Austria.
1706	(May 23) Defeat of French at Ramillies. (September 7) Defeat of French before Turin.
1708	(July 11) Defeat of French at Oudenarde.

1709	Peace Negotiations at The Hague.
	(June) Disgrace of Michel Chamillart as minister
	of war.
	(September 11) Battle of Malplaquet, where Allies
	win a pyrrhic victory.
1710	(February 15) Birth of Duke of Anjou, future Louis XV.
1711	(April) Death of Grand Dauphin, Louis's son.
1712	(February 18–20) Death of Duke of Burgundy, his wife,
	and one of his sons.
1713	(April 11) Peace of Utrecht.
1714	(March–September) Treaties of Rastadt-Baden.
	(July) Edict providing for succession of the royal
	bastards to the throne.
	(August 2) Louis makes his Will.
1715	(September 1) Louis dies.

PART ONE

LOUIS XIV VIEWS THE WORLD

Meticulous in matters concerning his household, Louis XIV kept a secret journal-memoir which he dictated to a reader, or lecteur. *His observations and exhortations were recorded in a loose-leaf notebook* (feuilles), *then edited and recopied into a* registre, *or copybook. Louis intended these notebooks to be both a manual for the instruction of his young son, the dauphin, or crown prince, born in 1661, and an apologia or defense of his reign. The king confided to his son that a prince owes an accounting of his actions "to the whole world and to . . . succeeding centuries", and yet cannot reveal his innermost thoughts to any of his contemporaries without giving away the secrets of his statecraft. Therefore Louis's observations were transmitted secretly to his heir and were perhaps never intended to be published. Fortunately for future historians his notebooks were not destroyed in 1714, when Louis burned many of his most secret papers, or when he was dying (Chapter 8). Instead they survived to be placed in the Royal Library.*

Louis throughout his Mémoires *exhorts his heir to recall that a prince's first duty is to God, to whom he will owe his ultimate accounting—He "alone is judge." Fortunately God has endowed princes with the invaluable gift of common sense, whose light will "break paths and uncover a thousand unexpected solutions." This same common sense opens the prince's eyes to those who might threaten his freedom of action: the priesthood, because they enmeshed the church in fruitless debate and ever threatened the land "with schism;" "corrupt ministers" and princes of the royal family who "become leader[s] of rebels," because they rob the prince of his gloire or reputation; and even women of his household because when given "liberty to speak to you of important things . . . they are bound to make us frail."*

But these dangers aside, the métier, *or appointed task, of being prince is noble, glorious and to be savored. A prince who takes his duties seriously—and Louis obviously did— will leave the kingdom augmented in size and power and*

will have thus added to his personal gloire and to the repu-
tation of the state.

Three short pieces, all written in Louis XIV's hand, serve
here as a coda to Louis "View of his World". The first,
"Reflections on the Rôle of the King," shows that Louis
was willing to sacrifice the career of a faithful minister,
Arnauld de Pomponne—a man whom Louis liked—for the
good of the State. The second selection, in the form of random "Instructions" to his grandson Philip V of Spain (the
Duke of Anjou), was written on the eve of the young king's
departure to Spain. "Never forget you are French," urged
his grandfather, but when you arrive in Spain, honor your
adopted countrymen: "See that your Viceroys and Governors
shall always be Spaniards." But above all, "Never allow
yourself to be ruled; be the master [!]" Lastly in a "Plan of
a Speech, 1710" Louis leaves both an apologia for France's
participation in the War of the Spanish Succession and what
may be construed as an open appeal to French public opinion for the support of his war effort.[1]

1

Louis XIV and the State: His Mémoires

Condition of France at the Beginning of Louis XIV's Personal Reign

I have given, . . . some consideration to the condition of
Kings—hard and rigorous in this respect—who owe, as it were,
a public account of their actions to the whole world and to all
succeeding centuries, and who, nevertheless, are unable to do so
to all and sundry at the time without injury to their greatest interests, and without divulging the secret reasons of their conduct.

[1] From Jean Longnon, ed., *A King's Lessons in Statecraft: Louis XIV:
Letters to His Heirs,* Herbert Wilson, trans. (London: T. Fisher Unwin Ltd.,
1924), pp. 40–45, 48–55, 64–75, 97–98, 102–3, 120–21, 126, 133–34, 142–45, 148–
51, 166–71, 173–76. Reprinted by permission of Ernest Benn Limited.

And, not doubting that the somewhat important and considerable affairs in which I have taken part, both within and without my kingdom, will one day exercise diversely the genius and passions of writers, I should not be sorry for you to possess in these Memoirs the means of setting history aright if it should err or not rightly interpret, through not having faithfully reported or well divined my plans and their motives. I will explain them to you without disguise, even where my good intentions have not been happily conceived, being persuaded that only a small mind and one usually at fault could expect never to make a mistake, and that those who have sufficient merit to succeed the more often, discover some magnanimity in recognising their faults.

I know not whether I should account as a fault of my own not to have assumed at the beginning the conduct of my realm. If it be a fault, I have striven earnestly to repair it afterwards, and I make bold to assure you that this was never the result either of negligence or of slackness.

From my early infancy the very name of *rois fainéants*[2] or *maires du palais* displeased me when mentioned in my presence. But I must point out the state of affairs: grievous disturbances throughout the kingdom before and after my majority; a foreign war in which these troubles at home had lost to France thousands and thousands of advantages; a Prince of my blood and of great name at the head of my enemies; many Cabals in the State; the Parliaments still in the possession and enjoyment of a usurped authority; at my Court very little disinterested fidelity and, on this account, my subjects, though outwardly most submissive, as much a responsibility and cause of misgiving to me as the most rebellious; a minister re-established in power despite so many factions, very skilful and very adroit, but whose views and methods were naturally very different from mine, whom, nevertheless, I could not gainsay, nor abate the least portion of his credit, without running the risk of again raising against him by some misleading appearance of disgrace those very storms which had been allayed with so much difficulty. I myself was still very young, though I had reached the majority of kings, which the State laws anticipate in order to avoid still greater evils, but not

[2] Weak kings.

the age at which mere private persons begin to regulate freely their own affairs. I only knew to its full extent the greatness of my burden, without having yet learned my own capabilities. Before all things, even before life itself, I placed firmly in my heart a lofty reputation, if so be I might acquire it, but I understood at the same time that my first moves would either lay its foundations or cause me to destroy all hopes of it for ever; and thus I felt myself almost equally being urged on and held back in my aims by the one and only desire for renown.

I did not, however, neglect to prove myself in secret and without a confidant, reasoning alone and in my heart over all events as they occurred, full of hope and joy when I discovered sometimes that my first views became those which men of skill and experience arrived at in the end; and I held firmly from the bottom of my heart that I should never have been placed and preserved on the throne animated by so great a passion to acquit myself well without being able to find the means to do so. Some years therefore having thus rolled by, the state of general peace, my marriage, my authority more firmly established, and the death of Cardinal Mazarin constrained me to defer no longer the putting into execution of the hopes and fears which I had entertained for so long.

Louis Takes the Reins of Government

I made a beginning by casting my eyes over all the different parties in the State, not indifferently, but with the glance of experience, sensibly touched at seeing nothing which did not invite and urge me to take it in hand, but carefully watching what the occasion and the state of affairs would permit. Everywhere was disorder. My Court as a whole was still very far removed from the sentiments in which I trust you will find it. Men of quality and officials, accustomed to continual intrigue with a minister who showed no aversion to it, and to whom it had been necessary, arrogated to themselves an imaginary right to everything that suited them. There was no governor of a city who was not difficult to govern; no request was preferred without some complaint of the past, or some hint of discontent for the future, which I was allowed to expect and to fear. The favours demanded, and extorted, rather than awaited, by this one and that, and always considerable, no longer were binding on any one, and were only regarded as useful in order to maltreat thenceforth those to whom they wished me to refuse them.

The finances, which give movement and action to the great organisation of the monarchy, were entirely exhausted, so much so that we could hardly find the ways and means. Much of the most necessary and most privileged expenses of my house and of my own privy purse were in arrears beyond all that was fitting, or maintained only on credit, to be a further subsequent burden. At the same time a prodigality showed itself among public men, masking on the one hand their malversations by every kind of artifice, and revealing them on the other in insolent and daring luxury, as though they feared I might take no notice of them.

The Church, apart from its usual troubles, after lengthy disputes on matters of the schools, a knowledge of which they allowed was unnecessary to salvation for any one, with points of disagreement augmenting day by day through the heat and obstinacy of their minds, and ceaselessly involving fresh human interests, was finally threatened with open schism by men who were all the more dangerous because they were capable of being very serviceable and greatly deserving, had they themselves been less opinionated. It was not a question only of a few private and obscure professors, but of Bishops established in their Sees and able to draw away the multitude after them, men of high repute, and of piety worthy of being held in reverence had it been accompanied by submission to the sentiments of the Church, by gentleness, moderation, and charity. Cardinal de Retz, Archbishop of Paris, whom for well-known reasons of State I could not permit to remain in the kingdom, encouraged all this rising sect from inclination or interest, and was held in favour by them.

The least of the ills affecting the order of Nobility was the fact of its being shared by an infinite number of usurpers possessing no right to it, or one acquired by money without any claim from service rendered. "The tyranny exercised by the nobles over their vassals and neighbours in some of my provinces could no longer be suffered or suppressed save by making severe and rigorous examples. The rage for duelling—somewhat modified by the exact observance of the latest regulations, over which I was al-

ways inflexible—was only noticeable in a now well advanced
recovery from so inveterate an ill, so that there was no reason
to despair of the remedy.

The administration of Justice itself, whose duty it is to reform
others, appeared to me the most difficult to reform. An infinity of
things contributed to this state of affairs: the appointments filled
haphazard or by money rather than by selection and merit; scant
experience and less knowledge on the part of some of the judges;
the regulations referring to age and service almost everywhere
eluded; chicanery firmly established through many centuries, and
fertile in inventing means of evading the most salutary laws. And
what especially conduced to this was the fact that these insatiable
gentry loved litigation and fostered it as their own peculiar property, applying themselves only to prolong and to add to it. Even
my Council, instead of supervising the other jurisdictions, too
often only introduced disorder by issuing a strange number of
contrary regulations, all in my name and as though by my command, which rendered the confusion far more disgraceful.

All this collection of evils, their consequences and effects, fell
principally upon the people, who, in addition, were loaded with
impositions, some crushed down by poverty, others suffering want
from their own laziness since the peace, and needing above all to
be alleviated and occupied.

Amid so many difficulties, some of which appeared to be insur-
mountable, three considerations gave me courage. The first was
that in these matters it is not in the power of Kings—inasmuch as
they are men and have to deal with men—to reach all the perfection they set before themselves, which is too far removed from
our feebleness; but that this impossibility of attainment is a
poor reason for not doing all we can, and this difficulty for not
always making progress. This, moreover, is not without its uses,
nor without glory. The second was that in all just and legitimate
enterprises, time, the fact of doing them even, and the aid of
Heaven, open out as a rule a thousand channels, and discover a
thousand facilities which we had not looked for. And the last was
one which of itself seemed to me to hold out visibly that help,
by disposing everything to the same end with which it inspired
me.

In fact, all was calm everywhere. There was no movement, nor
fear or seeming of any movement in my kingdom which might

interrupt or oppose my designs. Peace was established with my neighbours, and to all seeming for as long as I myself wished it, owing to the conditions of affairs then prevailing.

The Value and Pleasures of Hard Work

Two things without doubt were absolutely necessary: very hard work on my part, and a wise choice of persons capable of seconding it.

As for work, it may be, my son, that you will begin to read these Memoirs at an age when one is far more in the habit of dreading than loving it, only too happy to have escaped subjection to tutors and to have your hours regulated no longer, nor lengthy and prescribed study laid down for you.

On this heading I will not warn you solely that it is none the less toil *by which* one reigns, and *for which* one reigns, and that the conditions of royalty, which may seem to you sometimes hard and vexatious in so lofty a position, would appear pleasant and easy if there was any doubt of you reaching it.

There is something more, my son, and I hope that your own experience will never teach it to you: nothing could be more laborious to you than a great amount of idleness if you were to have the misfortune to fall into it through beginning by being disgusted with public affairs, then with pleasure, then with idleness itself, seeking everywhere fruitlessly for what can never be found, that is to say, the sweetness of repose and leisure without having the preceding fatigue and occupation.

I laid a rule on myself to work regularly twice every day, and for two or three hours each time with different persons, without counting the hours which I passed privately and alone, nor the time which I was able to give on particular occasions to any special affairs that might arise. There was no moment when I did not permit people to talk to me about them, provided that they were urgent; with the exception of foreign ministers who sometimes find too favourable moments in the familiarity allowed to them, either to obtain or to discover something, and whom one should not hear without being previously prepared.

I cannot tell you what fruit I gathered immediately I had taken this resolution. I felt myself, as it were, uplifted in thought and courage; I found myself quite another man, and with joy reproached myself for having been too long unaware of it. This first timidity, which a little self-judgment always produces and which at the beginning gave me pain, especially on occasions when I had to speak in public, disappeared in less than no time. The only thing I felt then was that I was King, and born to be one. I experienced next a delicious feeling, hard to express, and which you will not know yourself except by tasting it as I have done. For you must not imagine, my son, that the affairs of State are like some obscure and thorny path of learning which may possibly have already wearied you, wherein the mind strives to raise itself with effort above its purview, more often to arrive at no conclusion, and whose utility or apparent utility is repugnant to us as much as its difficulty. The function of Kings consists principally in allowing good sense to act, which always acts naturally and without effort. What we apply ourselves to is sometimes less difficult than what we do only for our amusement. Its usefulness always follows. A King, however skilful and enlightened be his ministers, cannot put his own hand to the work without its effect being seen. Success, which is agreeable in everything, even in the smallest matters, gratifies us in these as well as in the greatest, and there is no satisfaction to equal that of noting every day some progress in glorious and lofty enterprises, and in the happiness of the people which has been planned and thought out by oneself. All that is most necessary to this work is at the same time agreeable; for, in a word, my son, it is to have one's eyes open to the whole earth; to learn each hour the news concerning every province and every nation, the secrets of every court, the mood and the weaknesses of each Prince and of every foreign minister; to be well-informed on an infinite number of matters about which we are supposed to know nothing; to elicit from our subjects what they hide from us with the greatest care; to discover the most remote opinions of our own courtiers and the most hidden interests of those who come to us with quite contrary professions. I do not know of any other pleasure we would not renounce for that, even if curiosity alone gave us the opportunity.

I have dwelt on this important subject longer than I had intended, and far more for your sake than for my own; for while I am disclosing to you these methods and these alleviations attending the greatest cares of royalty I am not unaware that I am likewise depreciating almost the sole merit which I can hope for in the eyes of the world. But in this matter, my son, your honour is dearer to me than my own; and if it should happen that God call you to govern before you have yet taken to this spirit of application and to public affairs of which I am speaking, the least deference you can pay to the advice of a father, to whom I make bold to say you owe much in every kind of way, is to begin to do and to continue to do for sometime, even under constraint and dislike, for love of me who beg it of you, what you will do all your life from love of yourself, if once you have made a beginning.

I gave orders to the four Secretaries of State no longer to sign anything whatsoever without speaking to me; likewise to the Controller, and that he should authorise nothing as regards finance without its being registered in a book which must remain with me, and being noted down in a very abridged abstract form in which at any moment, and at a glance, I could see the state of the funds, and past and future expenditure.

The Chancellor received a like order, that is to say, to sign nothing with the seal except by my command, with the exception only of letters of justice, so called because it would be an injustice to refuse them, a procedure required more as a matter of form than of principle; and I allowed to remain the administering and remissions of cases manifestly pardonable, although I have since changed my opinion on this subject, as I will tell you in its proper place. I let it be understood that whatever the nature of the matter might be, direct application must be made to me when it was not a question that depended only on my favour; and to all my subjects without distinction I gave liberty to present their case to me at all hours, either verbally or by petitions.

At first petitions came in very great numbers, which nevertheless did not discourage me. The disorder in which my affairs had been placed was productive of many; the novelty and expectation, whether vain or unjust, attracted not less. A large number were presented connected with law-suits, which I could not and ought not to take out of the ordinary tribunals in order to have them adjudicated before me. But even in these things, apparently so unprofitable, I found great usefulness. By this means I informed myself in detail as to the state of my people; they saw that I was mindful of them, and nothing won their hearts so much. Oppression on the part of the ordinary tribunals might be represented to me in such a way as to make me feel it desirable to gain further information in order to take special measures when they were required. One or two examples of this kind prevented a thousand similar ills; the complaints, even when they were false and unjust, hindered my officers from giving a hearing to those which were more genuine and reasonable.

Choosing Ministers

Regarding the persons whose duty it was to second my labours, I resolved at all costs to have no prime minister; and if you will believe me, my son, and all your successors after you, the name shall be banished for ever from France, for there is nothing more undignified than to see all the administration on one side, and on the other, the mere title of King.

To effect this, it was necessary to divide my confidence and the execution of my orders without giving it entirely to one single person, applying these different people to different spheres according to their diverse talents, which is perhaps the first and greatest gift that Princes can possess.

I also made a resolution on a further matter. With a view the better to unite in myself alone all the authority of a master, although there must be in all affairs a certain amount of detail to which our occupations and also our dignity do not permit us to descend as a rule, I conceived the plan, after I should have made choice of my ministers, of entering sometimes into matters with each one of them, and when they least expected it, in order that they might understand that I could do the same upon other subjects and at any moment. Besides, a knowledge of some small detail acquired only occasionally, and for amusement rather than as a regular rule, is instructive little by little and without fatigue, on a thousand things which are not without their use in general resolutions, and which we ought to know and do ourselves were it possible that a single man could know and do everything.

It is not so easy for me to tell you, my son, what ought to be done in the choice of different ministers. In this matter fortune plays always, in spite of us, as large or a greater part than sagacity; and in the part that sagacity is able to play, intuition can do far more than taking thought.

Neither you nor I, my son, will seek out men for those kinds of employment whom distance or their own obscurity hides from our view, whatever be the capability they may possess. Of necessity, one must decide from a small number whom chance presents, that is to say, from among those who are already occupying some post, or men whose birth or inclination have placed nearest to us.

And for this art of knowing men, which will be so important to you, not only in this matter, but in all the occasions of your life, I will tell you, my son, that it is one that may be learnt, but cannot be taught.

In reality, it is doubtless right to take largely into account a man's general and established reputation, because the public is not consulted in the appointment, and cannot easily be imposed upon for long. It is a wise thing to hear every one, and not to believe entirely those who approach us with regard to their enemies over and above the good which they are compelled to recognise in them, nor with regard to their friends over and above the evil which they endeavour to excuse in them; it is still wiser to prove in small matters those whom one wishes to employ in greater. But the essence of the precepts for distinguishing clearly the talents, inclinations, and the tendency of each, is to make it a study and take pleasure in it; and this I exhort you to do, for, as a rule, from the smallest to the greatest things, you will never understand one of them if you do not make it a pleasure and like doing it.

In questions connected with the administration of justice, I communicated especially with the Chancellor, an officer of very long standing, and generally recognised as being very skilful in these matters.

I called him also to all the public Councils which I myself held, and particularly on two days of the week with the four Secretaries of State for the dispatch of ordinary affairs within the kingdom and for replies to petitions.

I also determined to be present sometimes at the different Administrative Councils held on my behalf, at which it was only a question of regulating matters between the various jurisdictions. And if more important occupations spare you the time, you will do well to use it sometimes in this way in order by your presence to encourage in their duty those taking part, and to become personally acquainted with the Magistrates who report and give their opinion on the cases. From this assembly the men are chosen, as a rule, for governorships of provinces, for Embassies, and for other great posts.

But as regards the most important interests of the State and secret matters wherein a small number of heads is to be desired as much as anything else, and which of themselves require more time and more application than all the rest put together, in my wish not to confide them to one minister alone I considered Le Tellier, Fouquet, and Lionne to be the three possessing the best capacity to serve them usefully.

The office of Secretary of State, which for twenty years had been exercised by Le Tellier with great devotion and assiduity, gave him a great knowledge of affairs. He had been employed all that time on most confidential matters. Cardinal Mazarin had often told me that he had recognised his capability and fidelity on the most delicate occasions, as had I too myself. His conduct was sagacious, prudent, and modest, on which I set great store.

Decision Making

Necessity reduces us to a small number of persons chosen from the rest, and whom it would not be politic to neglect. You will find out, moreover, my son, what I soon recognised, that by talking over our affairs when no other personal consideration should stand in our way, we learn not only much about others, but also about ourselves. The mind brings to fruition its own thoughts by giving them the light of day, whereas, before, it held them in confusion, undeveloped, and rough-hewn. Discussion, which excites and warms it, carries it insensibly from object to object further than solitary and silent meditation had done, and opens out a thousand fresh expedients from the very difficulties opposed to it.

Besides, our lofty position in some way separates us from our people to whom our ministers are closer, and are consequently able to see a thousand things of which we know nothing, but on which nevertheless we must make up our minds and take measures. Add to this their age, experience, deliberations, and their greater liberty to obtain information and suggestions from their inferiors, who in their turn gather them from others, step by step down to the lowest.

But when, on important occasions, they have reported to us all the aspects and all the opposing reasons, all that is done elsewhere in similar cases, all that has been done formerly, and all that might be done to-day, it is incumbent upon us, my son, to choose what must be actually done. And in regard to that choice I will make bold to tell you that if we do not lack good sense or courage there is no other who can make a better one than us; for to decide requires the *esprit de maître,* and without any comparison it is easier to do what one *is* than to imitate what one *is not.* And if we nearly always notice some difference between the private letters which we ourselves take the trouble to write, and those which our most skilled secretaries write for us, discovering in the latter a something less natural and the anxiety of a pen everlastingly in fear of saying too much or too little, have no doubt that in matters of the greatest consequence the difference will be still greater between our own resolutions and those which we leave our ministers to take without us; wherein, the cleverer they are the more will they hesitate from fear of the issue, and owing to their responsibility will sometimes become embarrassed for quite a long time over difficulties which would not have delayed us for a moment.

Wisdom directs that on certain occasions we allow much to chance. In such cases reason herself counsels us to follow some kind of blind motion or instinct above itself which seems to come from Heaven and is known to all men, but is undoubtedly of greater weight and more worthy of consideration in the case of those whom it has itself placed in the first rank. No one can say when we should distrust or obey this motion; neither books, nor rules, nor experience tell us; a certain appropriateness, a certain daring of the mind, always more unfettered in a man who owes no account of his actions to any one, enables us to discover this.

However this may be, and not to allude again to the subject, immediately I had begun this system of conduct with my ministers I knew very well, not so much from what they said, but from a certain air of truth which detached itself from flattery, just as a living person differs from the most perfect statue (and it came back to me afterwards in many unsuspected ways), that they were not only satisfied but somewhat surprised to see me not accepting entirely all that they advised on the most difficult questions, and, while I did not affect to disregard it, taking my part so unconstrainedly, and following the line which more often than not subsequent events clearly showed to have been the better. And though they saw very well from that time onwards that they would always hold the proper position of ministers with me and nothing else, they were only the more pleased at the situation in which they were placed, with its thousand other advantages, of entire security for doing their duty in it. For there is nothing more dangerous to men occupying positions such as theirs as a King who is usually asleep, and wakes up with a start from time to time after losing the thread of affairs, and one who, in this uncertain and confused light, blames everybody for their want of success, for chance mishaps, or for faults for which he should accuse himself.

Some Practical Measures for Reform

After having thus fully informed myself in private discussions with them I entered more boldly into practical action. There was nothing that appeared more pressing to me than to alleviate the condition of my people, to which the poverty of the provinces and the compassion I felt for them strongly urged me. The state of my finances, as I have shown you, seemed to oppose this, and in any case counselled delay; but we must always be in haste to do well. The reforms I took in hand, though beneficial to the public, were bound to be irksome to a large number of private people. It was appropriate to make a beginning with something that could only be agreeable, and besides, there was no other way of maintaining any longer even the name of peace without its being followed by some sort of sop of this kind as a promise of greater hopes for the future. I therefore put aside any other considerations and, as a pledge of further alleviation, I first remitted three millions of the taxes for the following year which had already been prescribed and were awaiting collection.

At the same time, but with the intention of having them better observed than heretofore, I renewed the regulations against wearing gold and silver on clothes, and a thousand other foreign

superfluities which were a kind of charge and contribution, outwardly voluntary but really obligatory, which my subjects, especially those most qualified and the persons at my Court, paid
daily to neighbouring nations, or, to be more correct, to luxury
and vanity.

For a thousand reasons, and also to pave the way for the reform of the administration of justice so greatly needed, it was
necessary to diminish the authority of the chief jurisdictions
which, under the pretext that their judgments were without appeal, and, as we say, sovereign and of final resort, regarded themselves as separate and independent sovereignties. I let it be known
that I would no longer tolerate their assumptions. The *Cour
des Aides* in Paris having been the first to exceed its duties and
in some degree its jurisdiction, I exiled a few of its most offending officers, believing that if this remedy were thoroughly employed at the outset, it would relieve me of the necessity of its
frequent application afterwards; and my action has been successful.

Immediately afterwards I gave them to understand my intentions still better in a solemn decree by my Supreme Council. For
it is quite true that these jurisdictions have no cause to regulate
each other in their different capacities, which are defined by laws
and edicts. In former times these sufficed to make them live in
peace with each other, or in the event of certain differences arising between them, especially in matters regarding private individuals, these were so rare and so little difficult of adjustment,
that the Kings themselves decided them with a word, more often
than not during a walk, on the report of the Magistrates, who
then consisted of a very small number, until, owing to the growth
in the kingdom of these matters and still more of chicanery, this
duty was entrusted principally to the Chancellor of France and
to the Administrative Council of which I have spoken already
to you. Now these officials of necessity should be fully authorised
to regulate the competence of the other jurisdictions (and also
all other matters of which from time to time we deem it suitable
for reasons of public utility or of our own proper service, to
give them cognisance exceptionally) by taking it over from them
inasmuch as they derive their power only from us. Notwithstanding, owing to this spirit of self-sufficiency and the disorder of
the times, they only yielded in so far as seemed good to them,

and outstepped their powers daily and in all manner of cases
in spite of their proper limitations, often enough going so far
as to say that they recognised the King's will in no other form
than that contained in the Ordinances and the authorised Edicts.

By this decree I forbade them all in general to give any judgments contrary to those of my Council under any pretext whatsoever, whether in their own jurisdiction or in their private
capacity, and I commanded them, when one or the other felt
they had suffered hurt to make their complaint to me and have
recourse to my authority, inasmuch as I had only entrusted to
them to exercise justice towards my subjects and not to create
their own justice of themselves, which thing constitutes a part
of sovereignty so closely united to the Crown and so much the
prerogative of the King alone that it cannot be communicated
to any other.

In the same year, but a little later, for I shall not observe
too closely the order of dates, in a certain matter connected with
the finances of all the record offices in general, and one which
they had never dared carry through in connection with those
of the Parliament in Paris, because the property belonged to the
officers of that body and sometimes to the chambers as a whole,
I made it be seen that these officers must submit to the common law, and that there was nothing to prevent my absolving
them from it when it pleased me to give this reward for their
services.

About the same time, I did a thing which seemed even too
bold, so greatly had the gentlemen of the law profited by it up
till then, and so full were their minds of the importance they
had acquired in the recent troubles through the abuse of their
power. From three quarters I reduced to two all the fresh mort-
gages which were charged upon my revenue, which had been
effected at a very extortionate rate during the war, and which
were eating up the best of my farms[3] of which the officials of
the corporations had acquired the greater part. And this made
them regard it as a fine thing to treat them as harshly as possible
in their most vital interests. But at bottom this action of mine
was perfectly just, for two quarters was still a great deal in return
for what they had advanced. The reform was necessary. My

[3] Tax farms.

affairs were not in such a state that I had nothing to fear from their resentment. It was more to the purpose to show them that I feared nothing they could do and that the times were changed. And those who from different interests had wished that these corporations might win the day learnt on the contrary from their submission what was due to me.

Vengeance to Be Avoided

In all these matters, my son, and in several others which you will see afterwards, which have doubtless mortified my officers of justice, I do not wish you to attribute to me (as might those who know me less) motives of harshness, hatred, or vengeance on account of all that happened in the Fronde, in which one cannot deny that these corporations often forgot themselves even to strange limits.

Their resentment, which at first appeared to be so just, may become less so if examined more closely. The jurisdictions have settled down of themselves and without trouble to their duties. The good servants have brought back the bad to better ways. Why impute to the whole body the faults of only a part, rather than the good service which has won the day? We should rather forget the one in favour of the other, and remember that, only to re-read history, there has hardly been any order in the Kingdom, Church, Nobility, Third Estate, which has not at some time blundered terribly and made amends.

Over and above this, my son, although in the matter of transgressions Kings are men as much or even more so than they are in other things, I do not fear to tell you that this is not so much the case when they are Kings in very truth, because an over-mastering and dominating passion, that of their interests, their greatness, and their glory, stifles every other in them.

The pleasure which people imagine to lie in vengeance is hardly meant for us. It only flatters those whose power is in doubt, and this is so true that even private individuals in whom there is something of uprightness have difficulty in exercising it upon an enemy altogether beaten down and one who can have no hope of ever raising himself again. In our case, my son, we are only very rarely in the condition of finding pleasure in taking revenge; for we have it in our power to do all things without constraint, or rather we find ourselves, on the contrary, in certain delicate and difficult positions which will not allow us to make trial of our power.

In short, as we belong to our people, so our people belong to us, and I have not yet seen that a wise man takes vengeance to his own prejudice by losing what belongs to him, under pretext that he has been ill served by it, instead of taking care to be better served for the future.

Therefore, my son, the resentment and anger felt by wise and skilful Kings against their subjects spring from nothing but justice and prudence.

The too great prominence of the Parliaments had been a danger to the whole kingdom during my minority. It was necessary to humble them, less for the evil they had already done than for what they might do in the future. Their authority, in so far as people regarded it as being in opposition to mine, produced very mischievous effects, however good their intentions may have been, and thwarted all my greatest and most useful measures. It was just that public utility should take the place of all other considerations, and reduce everything to their legitimate and natural order, even if (a thing which I have avoided nevertheless) it had been necessary to deprive this body of the power which had been given to it in former times; just as the painter makes no difficulty in effacing with his own hand his most daring and beautiful work every time he finds it overdone and in plain disproportion with the rest of his work.

But I know, my son, and can sincerely protest to you, that I had no aversion or rancour in my mind as regards my officers of justice. On the contrary, if old age in men is venerable, it appeared still more so to me in this so ancient a body. I am persuaded that possibly in no other branch of my State is the work so great, nor the rewards smaller. I have for all of them the affection and consideration that is their due; and you, my son, who, according to all appearances will find them still further removed from these former vain pretensions, should practise with all the more diligence what I myself do every day. I mean you should give them evidence on occasion of your esteem, you should know the chief representatives and those who possess the greatest merit, and let them see that you know them (for it is a gracious thing in a Prince to show that he is well informed on everything, and that duties performed far away from him are not lost); you should consider them and their families in the distribution of appointments and emoluments, and favour their plans when they wish to attach themselves more particularly to you, and in a word, accustom them to seeing you now and again by treating them well and giving them a friendly word instead of encouraging the practice of the past century when it was one of their understood rules not to go near the Louvre. And this was from no bad intention, but from the false idea of some imaginary opposition between the interests of the Prince and those of the people whose defenders they constituted themselves, not considering that these two interests are only one, that the tranquillity of subjects rests only on their obedience, that less harm results to the public by bearing with submission than by finding fault with even bad government by Kings, of whom God alone is the Judge, and that what they seem to be doing in opposition to the common law is more often based on reasons of State, which by universal consent form the first of all laws, but the least understood and the most obscure to all who do not govern.

Additional Practical Measures

The smallest moves were important in these first beginnings which were showing France what was to be the character of my reign and of my conduct for the entire future. I was hurt by the way in which it had become customary to treat with the Prince, or rather with the minister, and I nearly always made it appear doubtful what they might expect from my justice or benevolence.

The Convocation of the Clergy which had been sitting for a long time in Paris kept on putting off their departure, contrary to the expression of my wishes, until the issuing of certain decrees which they had demanded with insistence. I made them understand that they would gain nothing by these kinds of devices. They broke up, and it was only then that the decrees were issued.

As regards the governors of fortified places who so often abuse their powers, I first took away from them the financial subsidies which they had been allowed to levy during the war on the pretext of providing for the security of their cities without their having to wait for the money to be available, and of keeping them in good condition; but as these contributions amounted to vast sums in the hands of private individuals, they rendered them too powerful and too absolute. Next, without being noticed, and little by little, I placed fresh troops in nearly all the garrisons, no longer suffering them to be composed of men dependent upon them as formerly, but, on the contrary, of many who knew only me. And what could not have been dared or thought of a few months previously was brought about easily and quietly, all looking to me, and in reality receiving more legitimate and juster rewards for doing their duty. . . .

In a word, my son, I believed that, given the state of things, a little severity was the greatest kindness I could show to my people, a contrary disposition being bound to produce in them, of itself and in its consequences, an infinity of ills. For immediately a King slackens in what he has commanded, authority perishes, and with it all repose. Those who see a Prince at close quarters, and are the first to learn his weakness, are also the first to abuse it; after them come those in the second rank, and in the same way those in succession who hold some sort of power. The full weight falls upon the lowest ranks of the people, who by this means are oppressed by thousands and thousands of petty tyrants, instead of having a lawful King, whose indulgence nevertheless has been the sole cause of all this disorder.

The Problem of Glory

. . . I observed that, just as a Prince wins glory by overcoming difficulties he cannot avoid, so he incurs the risk of being accused of imprudence by throwing himself too lightly into those from which a little address might have spared him; that the greatness of our courage ought not to make us neglect the aid of our reason, and that the more dearly one loves glory, the more should one endeavour to win it surely; that under the pretext of the war with England I should so dispose of my forces and of my information as to make a more favourable beginning in Flanders; that the English by themselves need not be feared, but that their support would be of great weight in defending the territories belonging to Spain; that to attack these two powerful enemies simultaneously would be to form between them a *liaison* which could not be dissolved when I wished, and would infallibly compel me either to continue to fight them both at once, or to settle my differences with them under less advantageous conditions; that a union between Spain and England would promote the peace of Portugal; that, taking into consideration the present temper of the Dutch and their readiness to defend themselves, their help could not procure me as great advantages as the English could do me harm, and in my wish to take the future into consideration there was no more upright method of securing them in my interests than to allow my good faith to be visible to them by beginning the war solely on their behalf; but that at least I should appear glorious in the eyes of all the nations of the earth if, having my own rights to follow up on one side, and on the other, to protect my allies, I could show myself capable of neglecting my own interests to undertake the defence of those of others.

I was for some little time divided between these two views. But if the first flattered my mood more agreeably, the second touched my reason with greater force; and I felt that in the position in which I was situated I ought to do violence to my sentiments in order to attach myself to the interests of my Crown.

So I determined to undertake only the war on the sea, and in order to wage this more advantageously I wished to have the King of Denmark on our side.

The advantage which I saw in this was that by closing to the English the entrance to the Baltic Sea by his means, they would be deprived of all the commodities which they drew from it, and especially those things which were necessary on a voyage, and essential for conducting the war. The difficulty was that the Dutch, having quarrelled with that Prince, were demanding a certain sum to come to an agreement. But I arranged the matter by providing a portion of their claim from my own funds, and by means of this occasion I informed them in a secret Treaty of all the matters I required of them.

Self-control

From this example you may learn, my son, how essential it is for Princes to be masters of their angry feelings. On occasions of this kind which we can either dissimulate or take open notice of according to our choice, we should apply our minds not so much to consider the circumstances of the wrong we have re-

ceived as to weigh the exigencies of the times in which we are
living. When we become irritated unreasonably, it usually happens that while only thinking of wreaking our spite on him who
has angered us we do harm to ourselves also. From the empty
satisfaction we find in letting our vain anger break forth we
often lose the opportunity of obtaining solid advantages. The
heat which carries us away vanishes in a very little time, but the
losses it has caused us remain always present to our mind, together with the grief of having occasioned them by our own fault.

I know better than any one how greatly the least things
touching our dignity sensibly affect hearts which are jealous of
their glory. But, nevertheless, reason does not wish that one
should minutely take notice of everything, and perhaps it is also
conformable to the elevation in which we are placed sometimes
to neglect from noble motives what passes beneath us.

Exercising an altogether divine function here below, we ought
to appear incapable of perturbations which might lower it. Or if
it be true that our heart, in its inability to give the lie to the
feebleness of its nature, still feels, in spite of itself, vulgar emotions taking rise in it, our reason at least should conceal them so
soon as they are harmful to the public weal for which alone we
were born.

We never arrive at the end of vast enterprises without under-
going diverse difficulties, and if among them we find one which
obliges us in outward appearance to unbend somewhat of our
pride, the beauty which we hope from its success gives us sweet
consolation within ourselves, and the brilliant results which are
revealed in the end make glorious amends to us in the eyes of the
public.

The Granting of Favors

Wherefore, one might fairly reasonably ask whether a Prince
does not require as much ability to protect himself from the
different claims of his allies as to resist the attacks of his enemies.

In truth, any one taking into consideration the number of
desires, importunities, and murmurings to which Kings are exposed, would marvel less at seeing some of them agitated by such
a tumult of cries, and would find more worthy of esteem those
who, in the midst of these disturbances from without, preserve

within themselves that calm which is necessary to the perfect economy of reason.

Force of character assuredly is required to keep always the correct balance between so many people who are striving to make it incline to their side. Out of the vast number of neighbours surrounding us, of subjects who are at our bidding, of men who pay their court to us, of ministers and servants who give their counsel or wait upon us, there is hardly one who has not already formed in his mind some claim; and as each one of them is applying himself wholly to give an appearance of justice to what he is seeking, it is not easy for the Prince of himself, taken up as he is by so many other thoughts, to exercise always a perfect discernment between what is good and what is bad.

As regards this, it would be difficult to provide you with sure rules for the diversity of subjects which daily present themselves. But there are, however, certain general maxims of which it is well that you should be informed.

The first is that if you preserve towards all a universal complaisance you cannot nevertheless satisfy everybody, because what contents one always vexes several others.

The second is that one must not judge of the equity of a claim by the earnestness with which it is urged, because passion and self-interest have naturally more impetuosity than reason.

The third is that those who are in closest contact with you, and those whose advice you seek concerning the claims of others, are the very people over whose own requests you must take the greatest thought, or must consult people who are not of the same degree as they, from fear lest by taking the views of one concerning another's affair (even though they be not friends to each other) they may each favour the other reciprocally, having in their minds that the indulgence received by their comrade would be a good precedent for their own.

And lastly, the fourth is that one must always consider the consequences attaching to the request preferred rather than the merits of the man who prefers it, because the public good should always be placed before the satisfying of individuals, and no King in the world is so powerful that he will not soon ruin his State if he be determined to grant their requests solely to men of merit.

I am aware that one invariably gives offence to those whom one refuses, and that many always impute to the bad temper or the bad taste of the sovereign every difficulty presented by their request. It is also true that one always gives pain to oneself by rejecting the prayer of others, and that it is naturally pleasanter to draw gratitude to oneself than complaints. But in this matter, my son, we are obliged to sacrifice ourselves to the general welfare, and what is most vexing in this sacrifice is that although it costs us much it is little appreciated as a rule.

For, in reality, the greater number of those who distribute praise to Princes only set value on those virtues which are useful to them. The *beaux esprits* by profession have not always *belles âmes,* and in the (*belles choses*) which they utter in public they rarely refuse to take care of their own particular interests.

The Need for Good Advice

The advice given us does not bind us to follow it, except in so far as it seems reasonable; and, far from diminishing the proper sense of our own capabilities, it draws attention to it more surely than anything else, because all men of good sense are agreed that all the good that is done or proposed in the administration of the State must principally go to the credit of the Prince, and that there is nothing which brings his skill into better relief than when he knows how to secure good service and good counsel from his principal ministers.

There is this difference between the wise and imprudent monarch, that the latter will nearly always be badly served by the very people who pass for the most upright in the world, while the former will very often know how to obtain good service and good advice even from men whose integrity might be most open to suspicion.

For in reality, in everything which refers to the conduct of men one can establish a general principle that all have some secret leaning to their own particular advantage and that the virtue of the most upright people is with difficulty able to guard them against this natural movement if it be not sometimes supported by fear or hope. Even if some one exempt from this general rule be met, it is so singular a piece of good fortune that prudence does not allow one ever fully to be assured that he has really been found.

Considering things in this light according to their usual course, which makes men shun what is bad and seek after what is good according as they fear or hope, it is certain that an imprudent Prince who does not know how to bring all these great resources into play, and who listens to and treats equally all who are engaged in his affairs, almost as a natural consequence allows those very people who had applied themselves with the best intentions in the world to deteriorate in his service, because, as there is nothing to push them forward or to hold them back, they insensibly become slack or zealous according as their mood or interest dictates, scarcely ever giving a moment's reflection to their own conduct.

Instead, the most eager and the most interested in the service of an intelligent Prince dare not stray, however slightly, from the path they should keep, because they see him ever watchful over their actions, and fear, at the least deviation, to lose the esteem and trust which are always their first interest. They do not permit themselves any licence because they know that no fault will be hidden from him; they spare themselves in nothing because they are persuaded that no merit will fail to obtain the approval which is due to them in his sight. In a word, they carry out and advise always what they think is best because they are convinced that the favour, credit, and promotion to which they aspire, are only given in proportion to the zeal and fidelity which each one displays. . . .

Fear of Corrupt Advisers

Among corrupt ministers there are very few to be found so bold as openly to put their hands into their master's purse and appropriate directly the money over which he has given them the control, because that is a crime of which they could be too easily convicted. But the method of robbery which they find to be the most convenient, and which they believe to be safest against future investigation, is to take in another's name what they propose to gain profit from for themselves. The wiles which they practise to this end are of so many different kinds that I will not undertake to explain them to you in detail. But I will only tell you that they all have this in common that they always go on augmenting the theft which they have endeavoured to conceal.

In reality there is no doubt that the individual whose services the minister wishes to use in gaining these kinds of profits would never enter into the business unless he found some advantage for himself; and of necessity (under some form or another) the Prince, at whose expense this combination is arranged, bears at the same time both the burden of the unjust profit which his minister wishes to make and, in addition, the benefit to the other who provides the cover for this theft.

It is certain, furthermore, that in all these fraudulent conspiracies there are none which so much harms the Prince who suffers them as those in which foreigners are concerned, not only because the loss falls entirely on his own State, but also because it ruins his reputation with his neighbours, who recognise only too clearly by proofs such as these how little care or intelligence he gives to his affairs.

This consideration alone should, in my opinion, render more circumspect the unfaithful servants who carry on transactions of this kind, and at least it should teach their masters to be not content with examining men before taking them into their service, because the majority can easily disguise themselves for a time in view of attaining the authority they set before themselves, but also observe them still more carefully when they are actually in the management of affairs because, being then in the enjoyment of what they wish, they often follow their evil inclinations with greater freedom, the effect of which always falls upon the conduct of affairs or upon the reputation of their masters.

Such continual watchfulness will enable the Prince, by recognising accurately the weak spot in all who serve him, either to correct them with good advice according to their different characters, or to remove them when they are incorrigible, or even (if they have otherwise qualities to justify his putting up with them) so safeguard himself from the harm which their failings might do to his affairs, by taking pains to distinguish in their actions or proposals between what might be of good to his service and what proceeds from their evil propensities. . . .

Spending Public Funds

For while, on the one hand, I was continually working to reduce minor superfluous expenses, as I did this year by cutting down the contributions raised for the soldiers, by suppressing the greater number of the war commissioners and by suspending my building operations, . . . on the other I also spared no sums for important things, especially the increasing of the number of my friends or diminishing that of my enemies, in view of the weighty designs over which I was continually pondering.

If it is truly advantageous, my son, for the Prince to know how to be prudent with his money when the peaceful state of his affairs allows him the liberty, it is no less important that he should know how to spend it, even somewhat profusely, when the needs of his State require it or fortune offers him some special opportunity of exalting himself above his equals.

Sovereigns, whom Heaven has made to be the depositories of the fortunes of the public, are certainly acting in opposition to their duty when they scatter the substance of their subjects in unprofitable expenditure, but they are doing a still greater ill when by misplaced caution they refuse to disburse what may contribute to the glory of their nation, or the defence of their provinces.

It often happens that moderate sums dispensed at the right time, and with judgment, save States incomparably greater expenses and losses. Without any formal vote which can be cheaply acquired, it is sometimes necessary to levy large armies. A neighbour whom we could have made our friend with little expense sometimes costs us very dear when he becomes our enemy. The smallest number of enemy troops who are able to make a raid upon our States take from us in one month more than would have been required for the maintenance of secret intelligence service for ten years. And imprudent economisers, who do not understand these maxims, sooner or later meet with the punishment due to their miserly conduct, in wasted provinces, in the cessation of their revenues, in being abandoned by their allies, and in the contempt of their people.

Why make a difficulty in spending money on public necessities, since it is only to satisfy those needs that we have the right to raise it? To love money for money's sake is a passion of which fine souls are not capable; they never consider it as the object of their desire, but only as a necessary means to the execution of their designs. The wise Prince and the miserly private individual are absolutely opposed to each other in their conduct; the rich miser always seeks after money with avidity, receives it with extreme pleasure, saves it up without discernment, guards it apprehensively, and cannot spend the smallest portion without unbearable grief; whereas the virtuous Prince only imposes his levies

with restraint, exacts them with compassion, uses them with a
sense of duty, holds them in reserve only from prudence, and
never spends them except with altogether peculiar satisfaction
because he does this only to add to his glory, to increase his State,
or to benefit his subjects. . . .

The Prince as Arbiter

While on this incident I will take occasion to observe to you
how important it is for Princes to carry the greater part of their
own counsel in their own heads, and how momentous their words
often are as regards the success or ruin of their affairs. For although I am continually speaking to you here of my conversations with foreign ministers, I shall not pretend to counsel all
indifferently who wear crowns to put themselves to this proof
without having examined carefully beforehand whether they are
capable of emerging successfully therefrom. And I am of opinion
that those of moderate genius act more honestly and more safely
in abstaining from this function, than in being willing to display
their feebleness before the eyes of their neighbours, and thus endanger the interests of their provinces.

Many monarchs would be capable of conducting themselves
prudently in matters over which they had time to take counsel,
who would not be equal to upholding their affairs by themselves
in the face of skilful and experienced men, who never come to
them unprepared, and who always seek to take advantage of their
masters. Whatever notion of the subject to be treated may have
been given to us, a foreign minister is able at any hour, either
from chance or design, to propose certain things to us on which
we are not prepared. And notwithstanding this, what is annoying
is the fact that the false moves which the sovereign then makes
can only be disowned by his acknowledging his incapacity, and
they infallibly strike a blow either against the interests of his
State or his own reputation.

But it is not only in important negotiations that a Prince must
take heed of what he says. Even in the most ordinary conversation he is the more often in danger of failing. For he must guard
himself well from thinking that because a sovereign has authority
to do everything he also is at liberty to say everything. On the
contrary, the greater and more highly considered he be, the more

should he himself weigh what he says. Things which are of no account in the mouth of a private individual often become important from the sole reason that it is the Prince who has said them. Above all, the least mark of contempt he shows for a private individual cannot fail to do great harm to that man, because at the Courts of Princes every one is only esteemed by his fellows in proportion as they think he is esteemed by their master. And from this it happens that those who are offended in this way carry in their hearts, as a rule, a wound that only ceases with life.

There are two things which can console a man for stinging banter or a contemptuous word uttered by one of his fellows; the first is when he promises himself to find an opportunity soon to return a similar one; and the second is when he is able to persuade himself that what has been said to his disadvantage will not make an impression on those who heard it. But the man about whom the Prince has spoken feels his hurt all the more keenly because he has not any of these remedies. For if he dares to speak ill of his master it is only as a private individual, and it is not in his power to bring to his notice what he has said (which is the only balm in vengeance). Neither can he convince himself that what has been said about him has not been heard, because he knows with what delight the words of those in authority are received daily.

Wherefore I counsel you very seriously, my son, never to permit yourself any freedom in this matter, and to consider that affronts of this kind wound not only those who receive them, but also very often offend those who feign to hear them with the greatest applause, because when they see us holding in contempt those serving us just as they themselves, they fear with good reason that we may treat them in the same way on another occasion.

For, in short, you should take this as the foundation of everything, that to those occupying our rank nothing is pardoned. On the contrary, it often happens that quite indifferent remarks uttered by us without any design are applied by those who hear them either to themselves or to others of whom often enough we are not thinking. And although in reality we are not obliged to have particular regard to every impertinent conjecture, this should, however, compel us to be more cautious over our words in general in order at least to avoid giving any reasonable foundation to thoughts which might be formed to the prejudice of our service. . . .

Respect for Religion

I have never failed, when an occasion has presented itself, to impress upon you the great respect we should have for religion, and the deference we should show to its ministers in matters specially connected with their mission, that is to say, with the celebration of the Sacred Mysteries and the preaching of the doctrine of the Gospels. But because people connected with the Church are liable to presume a little too much on the advantages attaching to their profession, and are willing sometimes to make use of them in order to whittle down their most rightful duties, I feel obliged to explain to you certain points on this question which may be of importance.

The first is that Kings are absolute *seigneurs,* and from their nature have full and free disposal of all property both secular and ecclesiastical, to use it as wise dispensers, that is to say, in accordance with the requirements of their State.

The second is that those mysterious names, the Franchises and Liberties of the Church, with which perhaps people will endeavour to dazzle you, have equal reference to all the faithful whether they be laymen or tonsured, who are all equally sons of this common Mother; but that they exempt neither the one nor the other from subjection to Sovereigns, to whom the Gospel itself precisely enjoins that they should submit themselves.

The third is that all that people say in regard to any particular destination of the property of the Church, and to the intention of founders, is a mere scruple without foundation, because it is certain that, inasmuch as the founders of benefices when transmitting their succession were not able to free them either from the quit-rental or the other dues which they paid to particular *seigneurs,* so for a far stronger reason they could not release them from the first due of all which is payable to the Prince as *Seigneur* over all, for the general welfare of the whole realm.

The fourth is that if up till now permission has been given to ecclesiastics to deliberate in their assemblies on the amount which it is their duty to provide, they should not attribute this custom to any special privilege, because the same liberty is still left to the people of several provinces as a former mark of the probity existing in the first centuries, when justice was sufficient to animate each individual to do what he should according to his ability and, notwithstanding, this never prevented either laymen or ecclesiastics when they refused to fulfil their obligations of their own free will, from being compelled to do so.

And the fifth and last is that if there are dwellers in our Empire more bound than others to be of service to us as regards their property as a whole, these should be the beneficiaries who only hold all they have at our option. The claims attaching to them have been established as long as those of their benefices, and we have titles to them which have been preserved from the first period of the monarchy. Even Popes who have striven to despoil us of this right have made it more clear and more incontestable by the precise retractation of their ambitious pretensions which they have been obliged to make.

But we might say that in this matter there is no need of either titles or examples, because natural equity alone is sufficient to illustrate this point. Would it be just that the Nobility should give its services and its blood in the defence of the realm and so often consume its resources in the maintenance of the offices with which it is charged, and that the people (with so little substance and so many mouths to fill) should bear in addition the sole weight of all the expenses of the State, while ecclesiastics, exempt by their profession from the dangers of war, from the profusion of luxury and the burden of families, should enjoy in abundance all the advantages of the general public without ever contributing anything to its necessities? . . .

The Prince and the Army

This does not imply that I was not well aware that among people of humble condition from whom spring the soldiers and sometimes non-commissioned officers, the spirit of licentiousness is generally one of the principal motives which make men follow the military profession, and that not long ago there were commanders who over a long period maintained large armies with no other pay than liberty to pillage everywhere. But this example should only be imitated by men who have nothing to lose and have therefore nothing to preserve. For every Prince who cherishes his reputation with any feeling of decency cannot doubt that it is just as incumbent on him to protect the property of his subjects from being pillaged by his own troops as by those of his enemies. And he who gives heed to his affairs will not fail to perceive that all that he suffers to be taken from his people, in what manner soever this may happen, is never taken except at his own cost, because it is manifest that the more his provinces become exhausted, whether at the hands of soldiers or from any other cause, the less are they able to contribute to all the rest of the public charges. It is a great mistake for sovereigns to appropriate to themselves certain things and certain persons as if they belonged to them in any different way from the rest of what they hold under their empire.

The money in their privy purse, what is held in the hands of their treasurers, and what they leave in the commerce of their people, should all alike be managed carefully by them. The troops who are maintained in their own name are not for that reason more their own than those over whom they appoint individual commanders, and those who follow the profession of arms are not more bounden nor more useful in their service than the rest of their subjects.

Each profession in its own way contributes to the maintenance of the monarchy. The labourer provides by his labour food for all this great body; the artisan by his industry supplies all things serviceable to the convenience of the public, and the merchant collects from a thousand different places everything useful or pleasing produced by the entire world, in order to furnish it to every individual the moment he requires it; the financiers provide for the subsistence of the State by collecting the public monies; the judges, by applying the laws, maintain security among men; and the ecclesiastics, by instructing the people in religion, draw down the blessing of Heaven and preserve peace on earth.

For this reason, far from treating with contempt any of these callings, or favouring one at the expense of the others, we should be the common father of all of them, taking pains to bring them, if possible, to as great a degree of perfection as is suited to each, and we should hold the firm conviction that even the one to whom we might be disposed to show an unjust preference will feel no added affection or esteem for us, while the others will rightly complain and murmur.

If, however, notwithstanding all these reasons, you are unable to prevent yourself, my son, from cherishing that secret predilection which is nearly always held by generous souls for the profession of arms, take special care that this personal attraction never leads you to tolerate the excesses of those who follow it, and so act that your affection towards them may be seen in the care you exercise for their proper maintenance and welfare, rather than in allowing their morals to become corrupted. . . .

REFLECTIONS ON THE RÔLE * OF KING: 1679

Kings are often obliged to act contrary to their inclination in a way that wounds their own natural good instincts. They should like to give pleasure, and they often have to punish and ruin people to whom they are naturally well disposed. The interests of the State must come first. One has to do violence to one's inclinations, and not place oneself in the position of having to reproach oneself as regards any important matter which might have been done better had not certain private interests prevented it and turned aside the views one ought to have in the interests of the greatness, the welfare, and the power of the State.

There are often occasions which give trouble; some are delicate and difficult to disentangle; one's ideas are sometimes confused. So long as that is the case we can remain without coming to a decision; but the moment we have settled our mind upon anything, and think we have seen the best course, we must take it; that is what has often made me succeed in what I have done. The mistakes I have made, and which have caused me infinite trouble, have been caused by kindness, and by allowing myself to surrender too heedlessly to the advice of others.

Nothing is so dangerous as weakness, of whatever kind it be. To command others, one must raise oneself above them; and after having heard all sides one must decide on the judgment one may come to with an open mind, always keeping in view to order or do nothing unworthy of oneself, of the character one bears, or of the greatness of the State.

Princes who have good intentions and some knowledge of their affairs from experience or study, and great application in rendering themselves capable, find so many different channels for making themselves acquainted with them that they should exercise care over the individual and a general solicitude for all.

* Métier.

It is necessary to guard against oneself to beware of one's own inclinations, and to be always on the watch over one's natural self. The *rôle* of King is a great one, noble and pleasing when one feels oneself to be worthy of acquitting oneself well in all things undertaken; but it is not exempt from troubles, fatigue, and anxieties. Uncertainty sometimes makes one lose heart, and when one has spent a reasonable amount of time in examining into a matter one must come to a decision, and take the course one believes to be the best.

When one has the State in view, one is working for oneself. The good of the one makes the glory of the other. When the State is happy, eminent, and powerful, he who is the cause thereof is covered with glory, and as a consequence has a right to enjoy all that is most agreeable in life in a greater degree than his subjects, in proportion to his position and theirs.

When one has made a mistake one must repair it as soon as possible, and no consideration, not even goodness of heart, must stand in the way.

In 1671, a minister died who held a post of Secretary of State, the Department of Foreign Affairs. He was a capable man, but one not without his faults; he did not neglect to fill this post well, which is a very important one. I was some time considering to whom I should hand over his charge and, after having examined into the matter carefully, it seemed good to me that a man who had been serving for long in the Embassies was the one to fill it best. I sent for him; my choice was approved by every one, a thing that does not always happen. On his return I placed him in possession of his charge. I only knew him by reputation and through commissions with which I had entrusted him, which he had executed well.[4] But the work I had given him was too great and too extended for him. For several years I suffered from his weakness, his obstinacy, and his want of close attention. These cost me a good deal, and I did not profit by all the advantages I might have had—and all this was due to my kindness and good nature. Finally it was necessary for me to order him to resign because all that passed through his hands lost some of the greatness and authority which a man should possess when executing the orders of a King of France, who was no fool. If I had decided

[4] Arnauld de Pomponne.

to remove him sooner I should have avoided the inconveniences which have happened to me, and I should not be reproaching myself that my kindness to him had done harm to the State. I have mentioned this particular incident as an example of what I have said above.

INSTRUCTIONS TO PHILIP V: 1700

1. Never omit any of your duties, especially towards God.

2. Preserve yourself in the purity of your bringing up.

3. Cause God to be honoured in all places where you have power; procure His glory; give the example. It is one of the greatest forms of good that Kings can do.

4. On every occasion declare yourself on the side of virtue and against vice.

5. Have no attachment ever to any one.

6. Love your wife, lead a good life with her, and ask God to give you one suitable to you. I do not think you should take an Austrian woman.

7. Love the Spaniards and all your subjects attached to your Crowns and to your person; do not give preference to those who flatter you most; esteem those who for a good cause venture to displease you; these are your real friends.

8. Make your subjects happy; and, with a view to this, only engage in war when you are obliged, and after you have well considered and weighed the reasons with your Council.

9. Endeavour to keep your finances in good order; watch over the Indies and your fleets; keep your commerce in mind; live in close union with France, since there is nothing so advantageous to our two Powers as this union which nothing can withstand.

10. If you are compelled to go to war, place yourself at the head of your armies.

11. Take thought to re-establish your troops everywhere, and begin with those in Flanders.

12. Never leave your affairs for your pleasure; but make for yourself a rule of some kind which will give you occasions of liberty and distraction.

13. Of these there is hardly a more innocent one than the chase and the pleasure of some country house, provided that you do not incur too much expense thereon.

14. Pay great attention to your affairs; when people discuss them with you listen to them at length at the beginning, without deciding anything.

15. When you have attained to more knowledge, remember that it is for you to decide; but whatever be your experience, always hearken to all the advice and all the arguments of your Council before coming to this decision.

16. Do all in your power to get to know well the most important people, in order that you may make suitable use of them.

17. See that your Viceroys and Governors shall always be Spaniards.

18. Treat every one well; never say anything vexing to any one, but do honour to people of quality and merit.

19. Give evidence of your gratitude to the late King and to all who sided with choosing you as his successor.

20. Have great confidence in Cardinal Portocarrero, and show him your pleasure in the course he has pursued.

21. I think you should do something considerable for the Ambassador who had the tact to ask for you and to be the first to greet you in the quality of a subject.

22. Do not forget Bedmar, who has merit and is capable of being of service to you.

23. Have entire trust in the Duc d'Harcourt; he is a clever and an honest man, and will only give you advice in accordance with your interests.

24. Keep all Frenchmen in good order.

25. Treat your domestic servants well, but do not allow them too much familiarity, and trust them still less; use them so long as they are well-behaved; dismiss them on the least fault they commit and never uphold them against the Spaniards.

26. Have no dealings with the Queen Dowager beyond what you can help; arrange for her to leave Madrid and not to go out of Spain; wherever she is keep an eye on her conduct, and prevent her mixing herself up in any affairs; regard with suspicion those who have too much to do with her.

27. Love your relations always; keep in mind the grief they have had in leaving you; keep up a close intercourse with them in great things and small; ask us for anything you need, or wish to have, which you do not find where you are; we will do the same with you.

28. Never forget that you are French, and what may happen to you when you have made secure the Spanish succession with children; visit your kingdoms; go to Naples and Sicily; make a stay in Milan, and come to Flanders; this will be an opportunity of seeing us again; meanwhile visit Catalonia, Aragon, and the other places; see what is to be done for Ceuta.

29. Throw some money to the people when you are in Spain, and especially when entering Madrid.

30. Do not appear astonished at the extraordinary figures you will meet; never make fun of them; each country has its peculiar manners and you will soon become accustomed to what at first will seem most surprising to you.

31. Avoid as far as you can granting favours to those who give money to obtain them; dispense suitably and liberally, and be chary of accepting presents except they be trifling; if sometimes you cannot help accepting them, give a more valuable one to the donor after allowing a few days to pass.

32. Keep a privy purse in which to put your own money, of which you alone have the key.

33. I will end with one of the most important pieces of advice that I can give you: never allow yourself to be ruled; be the master; have no favourites or prime minister; listen to, and consult your Council, but do you decide yourself. God, who made you King, will give you the lights which are necessary to you, so long as you have a right intention.

PLAN OF A SPEECH: 1710

I have sustained this war with the high hand and pride which becomes this realm; through the valour of my Nobility and the zeal of my subjects I have been successful in the undertakings I have accomplished for the good of the State; I have given my whole concern and application to reach a successful issue; I have also put in motion the measures I thought necessary in fulfilling my duties, and in making known the love and tenderness I have for my people, by procuring by my labours a peace which will bring them rest for the remainder of my reign so that I need have no other care than for their welfare. After having extended the boundaries of this Empire, and protected my frontiers with the important strongholds I have taken, I have given ear to the proposals of peace which have been made to me, and I have exceeded perhaps on this occasion the limits of prudence in order to accomplish so great a work. I may say that I stepped out of my own character and did extreme violence to myself in order promptly to secure repose for my subjects at the expense of my reputation, or at least of my own particular satisfaction, and perhaps of my renown, which I willingly risked for the advantage of those who have enabled me to acquire it. I felt that I owed them this mark of gratitude. But seeing at this hour that my most vehement enemies have only wished to play with me and that they have employed all the artifices they could to deceive me as well as their allies by forcing them to contribute to the immense expenditure which their disordered ambition demanded, I do not see any other course to take than that of considering how to protect ourselves securely, making them understand that a France thoroughly united is stronger than all the powers they have got together at so great pains, by force and artifice, to overwhelm her. Up to now I have made use of the extraordinary measures which on similar occasions I have put into practice in order to provide sums proportionate to the expenditure indispensable to uphold the glory and safety of the State. Now that all sources are *quasi*-exhausted I come to you at this juncture to ask your counsel and your assistance, whence a safe issue will arise. Our enemies will learn from the efforts we shall put forth together that we are not in the condition they would have people believe, and by means of the help which I am asking of you and which I believe to be indispensable, we shall be able to force them to make a peace which shall be honourable to ourselves, lasting for our tranquillity, and agreeable to all the Princes of Europe. This is what I shall look to up to the moment of its conclusion, even in the greatest stress of the war, as well as to the welfare and happiness of my people which have always been, and will continue to be to the last moment of my life, my greatest and most serious concern.

2
The King's Advice to His Servants

This aide-mémoire *touches on a recurrent theme in Louis's correspondence: it is the prince's duty constantly to supervise and review his advisers' conduct in office. Louis XIV here weighs the evidence of misconduct of Louis François de Tellier, Marquis de Barbezieux (1668–1701), the secretary of state for war. The king is highly critical of Barbezieux's behavior: the secretary of state carouses, arises late, and (probably suffering from overindulgence) stays "forever away from his office"; he "speaks and writes crudely," and, above all, he delays bringing the king urgent letters from field commanders. Why, then, given the massive indictment, did Louis not dismiss Barbezieux? The answer, drawn from this hastily drafted, candid mémoire and from Louis's letters, reveals some of the principles by which he was guided in his relations with his ministers. First of all, Louis was extremely loyal to those who served him well, and to their families. Barbezieux's grandfather had been a distinguished Chancellor of France and his father a brilliant minister of war, and Louis did not want to betray his trust in the Le Tellier clan. Second, the king wished to maintain a balance of power within his high council (Conseil d'en haut). Barbezieux, being a Le Tellier, was destined like his father and grandfather to serve as a counterweight to the power of the other ministerial families, especially the Colberts. Third, Louis enjoyed "molding" his ministers to a preconceived image. Young (a minister at twenty-three) and impressionable, Barbezieux was malleable clay for the master potter's wheel. Lastly, from time to time Louis downgraded the power of a ministry, as he had done with the chancellory, the marine, and the controller-general's office. In the 1690's the war office underwent an administrative shake-up, leaving Louis for all intents as his own minister of war. This last point is underscored in Louis's letter to Vauban dated two years before Barbezieux's reprimand (see p. 52). The recipient of Louis's note is Sébastien Le Prestre de Vauban (1633–1707), the king's most famous military engineer, his commissary-general of fortifications, and an appointee of Barbezieux's father, Louvois. The king reminds Vauban that his advice will always be welcome and that he should send his letters to the king personally, thus by-passing the minister of war.*

TO THE ARCHBISHOP OF RHEIMS, CHARLES-MAURICE LE TELLIER [1]

Fontainebleau, October 29, 1695

That the life your nephew has been following while at Fontainebleau is not suitable [to a secretary of state]; that the public is scandalized by it;

That his secretaries relax their efforts, following his example;

That officers of state cannot find him in office when they wish to speak to him; that these officers waste time waiting for him;

That he is given to deceptions; that he is always flirting; that he prowls everywhere, never staying at home; that everyone thinks he does not know how to apply himself to his work, seeing him forever away from his office;

That he has delayed letters from Catalonia;

That he arises late, spending the night dining out, often with princes;

That he speaks and writes crudely;

That if he does not have a complete change of heart, it will be impossible for me to retain him as secretary of state;

That one must examine these charges so that one can counsel him, that is, after finding out what his [Barbezieux's] sentiments are.

That I would be sorry indeed to be forced to make changes but that I cannot avoid it;

[1] A *Mémoire* by Louis XIV to the Archbishop of Rheims, Charles-Maurice Le Tellier, while at Fontainebleau, October 29, 1695, to caution him concerning the displeasing conduct of his nephew [Louis François Le Tellier, Marquis de] Barbezieux, Secretary of State for War. From Pierre Gaxotte, ed., *Lettres de Louis XIV* (Paris: Jules Tallandier, 1930), p. 98; trans. J. C. Rule. Reproduced in English translation by permission of the publisher.

That it is impossible that his duties can go well with so little application;

That I wish he would change his ways without my having to say something to him;

That it is impossible that I could be deceived about so many wrong-doings, especially about his lack of application to his duties; that this carelessness has cost me much;

That, finally, one simply cannot have conducted oneself in a more intolerable manner than he has;

That some say that I am to blame for his actions, especially at a time like this [in the midst of the War of the League of Augsburg], when the greatest and most important affairs are in his hands;

That I could not excuse myself if I did not interfere in these matters for the good of the State; indeed it is the good of the State that exonerates me;

That I am warning him, perhaps too late, but so that he may behave in a manner proper to his family's position;

That I feel sorry for his family, and for the archbishop of Rheims in particular because of the affection and esteem that I have for the archbishop;

That he must make every effort to show his nephew the depths to which he has slipped and that he must agree to reform; that I do not want to lose the services of his nephew; that I have affection for him; but that for me, the welfare of the State comes before everything else;

That he would no longer respect me if I did not express my feelings;

That it is necessary to put an end to this one way or the other; that I want him to do his work well and apply himself completely; but that he cannot do this if he does not avoid the diversions which now distract him; he must do nothing else but carry out his duties which should occupy all of his time;

That such a life is distressing for a man of his age; but that it is necessary for him to make up his mind and to resolve not to forget any of these tasks and not to do anything which he himself will regret;

That he must stop the gossip at court by changing his conduct and that he must show me that he will not forget any of his duties, which presently are the most important in the kingdom.

TO VAUBAN [2]

Marly, June 13, 1693

I have received all the letters that you have written to me. Though I have not responded to each missive I am happy to say that I profited from the good ideas that they contained, even though my own plans do not always correspond with your thoughts. Do then continue to write to me about your ideas and do not be disheartened if I do not always follow your suggestions or respond regularly to your letters.

As for the misgivings I had about what the Duke of Luxembourg was doing [during the present campaign], I have ordered that they have some engineers ready [to be sent to the front] and have even sent Mesgringy on his way towards Namur. As for [the rest of] this year, I have no enterprise under way that demands your presence. That is why I have ordered Sousy to send on to you what I want you to do for the remainder of the summer, which conforms to the plans that I spoke to you about when you last took leave of me. After these matters are attended to you may return to Paris or home, which ever you prefer. That is all that I have to communicate for the present, assuring you that no one could have more esteem and affection for you than I have,

Louis

[2] Louis XIV to Vauban. From Pierre Gaxotte, ed., *Lettres de Louis XIV* (Paris: Jules Tallandier, 1930), p. 93; trans. J. C. Rule. Reproduced in English translation by permission of the publisher.

3
The King's Last Will and Testament

Like many mortals Louis XIV shunned mention of his own mortality. He hesitated making his last will, even when he had reached extreme old age. When he was seventy-six years old—and just one year before his death—he at last allowed his chancellor to draft a will. He did so for several pressing reasons. First, his senior ministers, especially Colbert de Torcy and Daniel-François Voysin, urged him to name a regency council that would limit the power of the Duke of Orleans by retaining in office Louis XIV's ministers and secretaries of state; second, Madame de Maintenon wished to secure the guardianship of the future king, Louis XV, for her favorite, the Duke of Maine; last, the king's confessor, Father Michel Le Tellier, implored Louis to place future ecclesiastical appointments in the hands of the confessor and two bishops. In drawing up his will Louis seemingly violates the principles of the administrative revolution of 1661 (see the selection, 165–68) by enlarging the King's Council to include several great noblemen. The reversal of policy, however, is more apparent than real: Louis XIV still excluded from the council all churchmen, allowed only two princes of the blood to sit, and included only loyal "political generals" Villeroy, Villars, Huxelles, Tallard, and d'Harcourt. Thus, in fact, the King's, or Regency, Council remained in the hands of the great bureaucrats and their friends.

Few documents reveal the innermost thoughts of a man more clearly than does a last Will and Testament; Louis XIV's will is no exception. He discloses his implacable abhorrence of "novelty" in religion, his fear of unruly nobility (as is shown in his prohibition on dueling); his love of his legitimized sons, the Duke of Maine and the Count of Toulouse; and his pride in having founded the retirement home for soldiers, the Invalides, and the girls' school at Saint Cyr.

*Seemingly Louis XIV intends by this First Codicil to his
Will, written only five months before his death, to further
safeguard the succession by appointing his faithful servant
and confidant François de Neufville, the Marshal of Villeroy, as governor of the future Louis XV. Villeroy, an important duke and peer of the realm, is immediately after the
death of Louis XIV to present the new king to the magistrates
and his fellow dukes and peers, solemnly assembled in the
great hall of the Parlement of Paris, where they will in the
presence of the new king read Louis XIV's Will aloud and
attest it. Then, in order to safeguard the young king and his
retinue, Villeroy is to conduct Louis XV to the safety of the
fortified château at Vincennes.*

*Saint-Simon's version of the "making of the Will" con-
tains continuous reference to the "they" who prevailed upon
Louis XIV to draft a Will in the first place. The "they" referred to by Saint-Simon included Madame de Maintenon,
her protégé and Louis XIV's legitimized son, the Duke of
Maine; and three of the secretaries of state, Daniel-François
Voysin, the chancellor; Colbert de Torcy, the foreign minister; and Torcy's cousin the controller-general of finances,
Nicolas Desmaretz. Together they wished to perpetuate the
influence of the "Old Court" into the period of Louis XV's
regency.[1]*

Marly, August 2, 1714

This is our last will and testament concerning the guardianship of the Dauphin, our great-grandson,[2] and concerning the
Council of the Regency that we wish to establish after our death,
during the king's minority.

Since, by the infinite mercy of God, the war which has, for
many years, troubled our kingdom with excursions and alarms
and which left us an uneasy legacy is happily terminated we
presently have nothing else at heart than to procure for our subjects the relief from the burdens that the war did not permit us

---

[1] The Last Will and Testament of Louis XIV. From "Testament of Louis
XIV and First Codicil", from Pierre Gaxotte, ed., *Lettres de Louis XIV* (Paris:
Jules Tallandier, 1930), pp. 174–83; trans. J. C. Rule. Reproduced in English
translation by permission of the publisher.

[2] Louis XV.

to give them, thus enabling them to enjoy the fruits of peace, and to remove all that which might be troublesome to their tranquillity. We believe, viewed in this perspective, that our paternal attentions should provide for and indeed anticipate as much as we can for the troubles which our kingdom may suffer, if, by the order of divine Providence, our death occurs before the Dauphin, our great-grandson who is the heir-apparent to our throne, has reached his fourteenth birthday, at which time he will come of age.

This is why we must provide for his guardianship, to take care of his education and to form, while he is still under age, a Council of Regency, capable by its prudence, its uprightenous, and by the great experience of those whom we will choose as members, of maintaining order in the government of the State, and of maintaining our subjects under the allegiance which they owe the young king.

This Council of the Regency will be composed of the Duke of Orleans, as head of the council, of the Duke of Bourbon, upon celebrating his twenty-fourth birthday, of the Duke of Maine, of the Count of Toulouse, of the Chancellor of France, of the President of the Royal Council, of the marshals of Villeroy, of Villars, of Huxelles, of Tallard and of d'Harcourt, of the four secretaries of state, and the controller-general of finances. We have chosen them because of the knowledge we have of their ability, of their talents, and of their faithful attachment that they have always shown us, and because we are satisfied they will show the same for the young king.

We want the young king to be under the guardianship and protection of the Council of the Regency; but since it is necessary that, under the authority of this council, someone of universally recognized merit and distinguished rank, be entrusted particularly with watching over the security, the guardianship, and the education of the young king, we appoint the Duke of Maine for this position and he is to commence this important function the day we die. We also appoint as governor for the young king, under the authority of the Duke of Maine, the Marshal of Villeroy, who, because of his good conduct, his honesty and his talents, appears to us to be worthy of this distinction, and of our esteem and our confidence. We are persuaded that, for all that which will relate to the person and to the education of the young king, the Duke of Maine and the Marshal of Villeroy, the king's governor, both animated by courageous feelings, will act in perfect accord and that they will omit nothing in order to inspire in him feelings of virtue, religion, and greatness which we want him to keep for the rest of his life.

We want all of the officers in charge of the king's guard and of his household to submit to the Duke of Maine and to obey him in everything he orders them to do, especially that relating to the security of the young king.

In case the Duke of Maine should die before us or while the king is under age, we appoint the Count of Toulouse to replace him, to have the same authority and to fulfill the same functions.

Likewise, if the Marshal of Villeroy dies before us or while the king is not yet of age, we appoint the Marshal of Harcourt to take his place as governor.

We want all business which must be decided by the authority of the king, without any exception or reservation: be it war or peace, the expenditure of monies and the administration of finances, or whether it be the choice of archbishops, bishops, or of [personnel] of monasteries and benefices, whose appointments must come from the young king, or appointments for the royal service, the secretaries of State, the controller-general of finances, all officers of war, the infantry troops as well as the galley officers, the officers of the magistracy as well as the superior courts and others, the officers of finance, the appointment of governors and lieutenant-generals for the king in the provinces within the kingdom, and those of commandant-majors in the citadels of the kingdom and along the frontiers within the kingdom, the appointments within the king's household, whether great or small, who are nominated by the king, and in general to all appointments, commissions, employments which the king must make, be proposed and determined by the Council of the Regency, and that the resolutions be taken by the majority of votes on the council, without permitting the Duke of Orleans, as head of the Council, alone, and by his special authority, to decide, to decree and to order, and to dispatch any order, in the name of the young king, other than by following the [majority] decision of the Council of the Regency.

If it happens that there are, on some affairs, a diversity of opinions among the council members, those who are present are obligated to reassemble and vote again: the majority will always decide; but if it should be found that upon the second vote there is an equal number of votes for each side, in this case only, the opinion of the Duke of Orleans, as head of the council, will prevail.

When it comes time to appoint people for religious benefices, the king's confessor will go to the council and present the list of vacancies for these benefices and suggest the people who would be capable of filling them. There will be admitted to the same council, when it is time to nominate for the benefices, two archbishops or bishops, from those at court, who will be summoned by the order of the Council of the Regency, in order to come and give them their advice on the choice of the names proposed.

The Council of the Regency will assemble four or five days a week, in the mornings, in the king's apartment or the king's cabinet; as soon as the king is ten years old, he may be present when he wishes, not to decide and give orders, but to listen and to form his first ideas of affairs of state.

In case the Duke of Orleans is absent or delayed, he who is next in rank will conduct the council so that the course of business will not be interrupted, and if there is an equal division of votes, his vote will prevail.

An account will be kept by the senior of the secretaries of State, who is present at the council, of everything which will have been deliberated on and resolved in order that these decisions may be converted afterwards into dispatches to be sent out in the king's name.

If, before we die, one of the people we have appointed to be a member of the Council of the Regency dies or is incapable of completing his term, we reserve the power to appoint another person to replace him and we will do it by a decree that will be written entirely by our hand and which will likewise not appear until after our death; and if we do not appoint anyone, the number of the members of the Council of the Regency will be restricted to those who are living the day of our death.

There will not be any change made in the Council of the Regency during the king's minority; and if, during that minority, one of the people whom we have appointed is unable to participate, the vacancy will be filled by the choice and deliberation of the Council of the Regency, without changing the number of those who are to compose it, such as it is the day of our death; and in case it should happen that some members cannot attend, because of illness or another reason, there must always be at least seven people, of those who have been appointed as members, so that the deliberations which have been taken will have their entire force and authority; and, for that purpose, in all the edicts, declarations, letters patent, provisions and acts which must be deliberated by the Council of the Regency and who dispatch them while the king is under age, there will be mentioned a precise count of the number of members who attended the council meeting, where the edicts, declarations, letters patent and other dispatches will be deliberated.

Our principal goal throughout our reign has always been to conserve for our kingdom the purity of the Roman Catholic religion, banishing all sorts of novelty and making every effort to reunite within the Church those who had left it. Our intention is that the Council of the Regency adhere to the policy of maintaining the laws and regulations we have made concerning this subject and we encourage the Dauphin, our great-grandson, when he comes of age never to allow any outrage to be perpetrated against the Church and to maintain with the same firmness [as his predecessors] the laws against dueling as the most necessary and useful way of gaining God's blessing for our posterity and that of our kingdom, and for the preservation of the nobility, who have been our main strength.

Our intention is that the arrangements contained in our edict of the month of July last, made in favor of the Duke of Maine and the Count of Toulouse and their descendants, have forever its full force of law, without at any time revoking that which we have declared to be our desire.

Among the different establishments which we have made during our reign, there is none which could be more useful to the State than the Royal Hôtel des Invalides [old soldiers' home]. It is only fair that the soldiers who, because of the wounds they received during the war, or because of their long term of service and their age, are unable to work or earn their living, be assured of sustenance for the rest of their lives. Many officers who have lost their personal fortunes can also find an honorable retreat there. The Dauphin and every king who succeeds us must take it as an all-sacred pledge to maintain this establishment and to accord it a particular protection; we urge this as much as is in our power to do.

The endowment which we have made for a house at Saint-Cyr for the education of two hundred and fifty young ladies will in the future give our successors a means of bestowing favors on many families of the nobility in our kingdom who, finding themselves burdened with many children and with little wealth, would regret not being able to furnish the necessary expenditures in order to give their children an education fitting their birth. We wish that if, in our lifetime, the 50,000 *livres* of revenue from land which we have given for the endowment is not entirely replenished, then it be taken from new acquisitions as soon as possible after our death in order to make up for that which is lacking, and that the other sums which we have assigned to the building of this foundation out of our properties and general receipts as much as for increasing the endowment as for ensuring a dowry for the young ladies who graduate when twenty years old, be regularly paid; so that in no case or under no pretext which might be made can our endowment be diminished, and so that no harm might be done to the agreement which has been made from the income of the abbey of Saint Denis, likewise that nothing be changed in the rules which we have judged appropriate for their household management, and for the quality of the proofs which must be given by the young ladies to receive a position in the home.

We have no other plans, in the disposition of our present will, except for the well-being of our State and our subjects. We beseech God to bless our posterity and to grant us the favor of being useful for the rest of our lives, in order to erase our sins and to obtain His mercy.

FIRST CODICIL

Versailles, April 13, 1715

By my will deposited in Parlement, I have appointed the Marshal of Villeroy as governor for the Dauphin and I have indicated what are to be his authority and his functions. My intention is that, from the moment of my death until my will has been opened, he have all authority over the officers of the household of the young king and over the troops which compose it; that he order the said troops, immediately after my death, to go to the place where the young king will be staying, in order to bring him to Vincennes, where the air is better.

The young king, on his way to Vincennes, shall pass through Paris and shall go to Parlement,[2] in order to open my will in the presence of the princes, peers, and others who have the right and who will wish to be there. During the procession and the meeting of the young king in Parlement, the Marshal of Villeroy shall give all of the commands so that the life guards, the French and Swiss guards, may take their posts in the streets and the palace, which is the custom when kings go to Parlement; this is done so that everything may occur with the proper security and dignity.

After my will has been opened and read, the Marshal of Villeroy shall lead the young king with his household to Vincennes, where he shall remain for as long as the Council of the Regency judges fitting and appropriate. The Marshal of Villeroy shall have the title of governor, following that which is dictated in my will; he shall watch over the conduct of the young king until he has had his seventh birthday; the Duchess of Ventadour shall remain, as is the custom, governess and charged with the same duties which she has performed until the present.

I appoint as vice-governor Sommery, who has already held this post for my grandson the Dauphin, and Geoffreville lieutenant-general of my armies. Moreover, I confirm all which is in my will, so that everything which it contains be accomplished.

SAINT-SIMON'S ACCOUNT OF THE MAKING OF LOUIS XIV'S WILL [3]

The Court at that time was at Versailles. On Sunday, 26 August [1714], Mesmes the premier président and Daguesseau the procureur général entered the study after the King's *lever;* they had already seen the Chancellor, and had agreed on the means to safeguard the precious testament. You may be sure that as soon as

[2] In this context the Parlement of Paris signifies a plenary meeting of the higher judges of the Parlement and the dukes and peers of the realm, to attest Louis XIV's will.

[3] From *Historical Memoirs of the Duc de Saint-Simon* (London: Hamish Hamilton, 1968) II, 353–54, edited and trans. Lucy Norton. Reprinted by permission of the publisher.

M. du Maine had secured his document he had discussed it thoroughly with his tool, the premier président. When they were alone, the King pulled open a drawer and took from it a large packet sealed with seven seals—I do not know whether M. du Maine, when he had it so sanctified, was thinking of that mysterious Book of the Seven Seals which is mentioned in the Apocrypha. However that may be, the King handed them the package, saying, "Messieurs, this is my will; no one but myself knows its contents; to your care I consign it for safe keeping by the Parlement, to whom I can show no higher proof of my trust and esteem. The fate of the wills of earlier kings and of my royal father makes me well aware what may become of it. But they would have it. They pestered me. They gave me no peace, no matter what I said to them. Now at least I have earned my rest. Here it is! Take it now! Come what may, I shall have peace of mind and hear no more of it." Then, turning on his heel with a curt nod, he went into another room, leaving them almost petrified with fright. They gazed at one another, deeply alarmed by what they had heard and by the King's look and expression, and as soon as they had come to their senses they left and returned to Paris. It was not known until after dinner that the King had made a will and had given it into their keeping. As the news spread, the entire Court was filled with dismay; but the toadies, who were at heart as deeply shocked as the rest, surpassed themselves in praise and eulogies.

On the following day, 27 May, the Queen of England came from Chaillot, where she spent most of her time, to visit Mme de Maintenon. The King went in to see her, but no sooner did he clap eyes on her than he burst out with, "Madame, I have made a will; they badgered me until it was done," then, turning to Mme de Maintenon, "I have bought my rest now. I realize the futility of it all; we may do as we wish while we live; afterwards we have less power than ordinary folk. You have only to think what happened to my royal father's will—and that immediately after he died. I knew all this; but they would have it; they gave me no peace. Well! Madame, I have done it now; perhaps it may have some influence. At least they will stop tormenting me."

Words so expressive of the King's outraged feelings, and of the long and bitter struggle before he yielded from misery and exhaustion—words so plain and so momentous—require proof of

authenticity. Here it is! What the King said to the premier président and the procureur général, I learned from the former, who
could never forget it. It is true, for I must be quite accurate, that
he told me a long time afterwards; but he then repeated the
King's speech to me, word for word, as I have written it here.

PART TWO

LOUIS XIV VIEWED BY HIS CONTEMPORARIES

Louis XIV had lived too long and touched the lives of too many people not to become a figure of controversy among succeeding generations of historians. The first school of historical critics appeared even before Louis's death, led by Archbishop Fénelon (Chapter 7) and the Duke of Saint-Simon (Chapter 4).

Like Louis XIV, Louis de Rouvroy, the Duke of Saint-Simon (1675–1755) was a master of detail. His pen sketches of the great and near-great of the French court, distilled from masses of disparate evidence and recorded in his vast Mémoires, furnish us with an incomparable picture of the last years of the "great century." The little duke, who was inordinately proud of his noble lineage, became a celebrated defender of the aristocratic principle of government, or what has become known as the thèse nobiliaire. He stoutly opposed Louis XIV's refusal to admit the great nobles to his councils, disliked the fact that the king listened to advice from the basest of servants—even valets; that he selected his ministers from among the "vile bourgeois"; and favored his illegitimate children. Louis XIV had the makings of a great king, said Saint-Simon, had he not been "drowned in vanity."

Saint-Simon observes in the first brief selection that though Louis XIV grew up "amidst . . . continual upheavals . . ." the "tender and skillful" care taken of him by Anne of Austria and Mazarin allowed him to survive the worst excesses of the Frondes. In the second selection Saint-Simon spins out more finely the "Character of the King."

4

General Character and Education

THE EDUCATION OF FATHER AND SON COMPARED [1]

When one considers that both Louis XIII and Louis XIV were long kept in ignorance and thus in lead strings, we may say that their educations were similar. Basically, however, their educations differed greatly both [as to the setting] and the general outlook of their tutors. The father, Louis XIII, was humbled at every turn by his tutors, more aptly called petty tyrants; the son, Louis XIV, on the contrary, was only kept out of mischief and otherwise was left to his own devices, being allowed to enjoy those past-times that seemed neither to sharpen nor to dull his mind. The father for many years of his life saw no foreign wars, and until the death of Marshal d'Ancre[2] witnessed no great domestic upheavals. The son, on the other hand, was born and raised in the heat of [one of France's] bitterest foreign wars and most distressing civil wars, both of which caused the young king and his court to move from place to place across the kingdom. Growing up amidst these continual upheavals it was impossible that Louis XIV should not hear the distressing events of the day discussed and be affected by what he heard, even though the queen mother and Mazarin took care to shield him. The tender and skillful way in which the cardinal and the queen mother treated Louis caused him to long remain submissive to them, although he could not have remained unaware of how he was being kept in lead strings. Their kindness, however, smothered the bitterness of restraint. Louis was fond of the cardinal and felt an especial tenderness toward his mother. He allowed them to govern as they pleased without challenging them. We can see, then, that though the father and son were much alike, nothing

---

[1] From *Écrits inédits de Saint-Simon*, ed. M. P. Faugère, 8 vols. (Paris: Plon et Cie, 1880–93), Vol. I, pp. 14–15. Translated by John C. Rule.

[2] Marie de Medici's chief adviser, assassinated in 1617.

could have been different than the years leading up to the moment that each began his personal rule.

THE CHARACTER OF LOUIS XIV [3]

I shall pass over the stormy period of Louis XIV's minority. At twenty-three years of age he entered the great world as King, under the most favourable auspices. His ministers were the most skillful in all Europe; his generals the best; his Court was filled with illustrious and celver men, formed during the troubles which had followed the death of Louis XIII.

Louis XIV was made for a brilliant Court. In the midst of other men, his figure, his courage, his grace, his beauty, his grand mien, even the tone of his voice and the majestic and natural charm of all his person, distinguished him till his death as the King Bee, and showed that if he had only been born a simple private gentleman, he would equally have excelled in fêtes, pleasures, and gallantry, and would have had the greatest success in love. The intrigues and adventures which early in life he had been engaged in—when the Comtesse de Soissons lodged at the Tuileries, as superintendent of the Queen's household, and was the centre figure of the Court group—had exercised an unfortunate influence upon him: he received those impressions with which he could never after successfully struggle. From this time, intellect, education, nobility of sentiment, and high principle, in others, became objects of suspicion to him, and soon of hatred. The more he advanced in years the more this sentiment was confirmed in him. He wished to reign by himself. His jealousy on this point unceasingly became weakness. He reigned, indeed, in little things; the great he could never reach: even in the former, too, he was often governed. The superior ability of his early ministers and his early generals soon wearied him. He liked nobody to be in any way superior to him. Thus he chose his ministers, not for their knowledge, but for their ignorance; not for their capacity, but for their want of it. He liked to form them, as he said; liked to teach them even the most trifling things. It was the same with his generals. He took credit to himself for instructing them;

[3] From *The Memoirs of the Duke of Saint-Simon* . . . , trans. Bayle St. John 2 vols. (New York: Willey Book Company, 1901), Vol. II, pp. 216–19; 223–28; 230–33.

wished it to be thought that from his cabinet he commanded and directed all his armies. Naturally fond of trifles, he unceasingly occupied himself with the most petty details of his troops, his household, his mansions; would even instruct his cooks, who received, like novices, lessons they had known by heart for years. This vanity, this unmeasured and unreasonable love of admiration, was his ruin. His ministers, his generals, his mistresses, his courtiers, soon perceived his weakness. They praised him with emulation and spoiled him. Praises, or to say truth, flattery, pleased him to such an extent, that the coarsest was well received, the vilest even better relished. It was the sole means by which you could approach him. Those whom he liked owed his affection for them, to their untiring flatteries. This is what gave his ministers so much authority, and the opportunities they had for adulating him, of attributing everything to him, and of pretending to learn everything from him. Suppleness, meanness, an admiring, dependent, cringing manner—above all, an air of nothingness— were the sole means of pleasing him.

This poison spread. It spread, too, to an incredible extent, in a prince who, although of intellect beneath mediocrity, was not utterly without sense, and who had had some experience. Without voice or musical knowledge, he used to sing, in private, the passages of the opera prologues that were fullest of his praises! He was drowned in vanity; and so deeply, that at his public suppers—all the Court present, musicians also—he would hum these self-same praises between his teeth, when the music they were set to was played!

And yet, it must be admitted, he might have done better. Though his intellect, as I have said, was beneath mediocrity, it was capable of being formed. He loved glory, was fond of order and regularity; was by disposition prudent, moderate, discreet, master of his movements and his tongue. Will it be believed? He was also by disposition good and just! God had sufficiently gifted him to enable him to be a good King; perhaps even *a tolerably great King!* All the evil came to him from elsewhere. His early education was . . . neglected. . . . He has often been heard to speak of those times with bitterness, and even to relate that, one evening he was found in the basin of the Palais Royale garden fountain, into which he had fallen! He was scarcely taught how to read or write, and remained so ignorant, that the most familiar historical and other facts were utterly unknown to him! He fell, accordingly, and sometimes even in public, into the grossest absurdities.

It was his vanity, his desire for glory, that led him, soon after the death of the King of Spain, to make that event the pretext for war; in spite of the renunciations so recently made, so carefully stipulated, in the marriage contract. He marched into Flanders; his conquests there were rapid; the passage of the Rhine was admirable; the triple alliance of England, Sweden, and Holland only animated him. In the midst of winter he took Franche-Comté, by restoring which at the peace of Aix-la-Chapelle, he preserved his conquests in Flanders. All was flourishing then in the state. Riches everywhere. Colbert had placed the finances, the navy, commerce, manufactures, letters even, upon the highest point; and this age, like that of Augustus, produced in abundance illustrious men of all kinds,—even those illustrious only in pleasures.

Le Tellier and Louvois, his son, who had the war department, trembled at the success and at the credit of Colbert, and had no difficulty in putting into the head of the King a new war, the success of which caused such fear to all Europe that France never recovered from it, and after having been upon the point of succumbing to this war, for a long time felt the weight and misfortune of it. Such was the real cause of that famous Dutch war. . . .

Thus, we see this monarch, grand, rich, conquering, the arbiter of Europe; feared and admired as long as the ministers and captains existed who really deserved the name. When they were no more, the machine kept moving some time by impulsion, and from their influence. But soon afterwards we saw beneath the surface; faults and errors were multiplied, and decay came on with giant strides; without, however, opening the eyes of that despotic master, so anxious to do everything and direct everything himself, and who seemed to indemnify himself for disdain abroad by increasing fear and trembling at home.

So much for the reign of this vain-glorious monarch.

Let me touch now upon some other incidents in his career, and upon some points in his character.

Setting for Royalty

He early showed a disinclination for Paris. The troubles that had taken place there during his minority made him regard the place as dangerous; he wished, too, to render himself venerable by hiding himself from the eyes of the multitude; all these considerations fixed him at Saint-Germain soon after the death of the Queen, his mother. It was to that place he began to attract the world by fêtes and gallantries, and by making it felt that he wished to be often seen.

These excursions of Louis XIV by degrees gave birth to those immense buildings he erected at Versailles; and their convenience for a numerous court, so different from the apartments at Saint-Germain, led him to take up his abode there entirely shortly after the death of the Queen. He built an infinite number of apartments, which were asked for by those who wished to pay their court to him; whereas at Saint-Germain nearly everybody was obliged to lodge in the town, and the few who found accommodation at the château were strangely inconvenienced.

The frequent fêtes, the private promenades at Versailles, the journeys, were means on which the King seized in order to distinguish or mortify the courtiers, and thus render them more assiduous in pleasing him. He felt that of real favours he had not enough to bestow; in order to keep up the spirit of devotion, he therefore unceasingly invented all sorts of ideal ones, little preferences and petty distinctions, which answered his purpose as well.

He was exceedingly jealous of the attention paid him. Not only did he notice the presence of the most distinguished courtiers, but those of inferior degree also. He looked to the right and to the left, not only upon rising but upon going to bed, at his meals, in passing through his apartments, or his gardens of Versailles, where alone the courtiers were allowed to follow him; he saw and noticed everybody; not one escaped him, not even those who hoped to remain unnoticed. He marked well all absentees from the Court, found out the reason of their absence, and never lost an opportunity of acting towards them as the occasion might seem to justify. With some of the courtiers (the most distinguished), it was a demerit not to make the Court their ordinary abode; with others 'twas a fault to come but rarely; for those who never or scarcely ever came it was certain disgrace. When their names were in any way mentioned, "I do not know them," the King would reply haughtily. Those who presented themselves but seldom were thus characterised: "They are people I never see;" these decrees were irrevocable. He could not bear people who liked Paris.

Royal Omniscience

Louis XIV took great pains to be well informed of all that passed everywhere; in the public places, in the private houses, in society and familiar intercourse. His spies and tell-tales were infinite. He had them of all species; many who were ignorant that their information reached him; others who knew it; others who wrote to him direct, sending their letters through channels he indicated; and all these letters were seen by him alone, and always before everything else; others who sometimes spoke to him secretly in his cabinet, entering by the back stairs. These unknown means ruined an infinite number of people of all classes, who never could discover the cause; often ruined them very unjustly; for the King, once prejudiced, never altered his opinion, or so rarely, that nothing was more rare. He had, too, another fault, very dangerous for others and often for himself, since it deprived him of good subjects. He had an excellent memory; in this way, that if he saw a man who, twenty years before, perhaps, had in some manner offended him, he did not forget the man, though he might forget the offence. This was enough, however, to exclude the person from all favour. The representations of a minister, of a general, of his confessor even, could not move the King. He would not yield.

The most cruel means by which the King was informed of what was passing—for many years before anybody knew it—was that of opening letters. The promptitude and dexterity with which they were opened passes understanding. He saw extracts from all the letters in which there were passages that the chiefs of the post-office, and then the minister who governed it, thought ought to go before him; entire letters, too, were sent to him, when their contents seemed to justify the sending. Thus the chiefs of the post, nay, the principal clerks were in a position to suppose what they pleased and against whom they pleased. A word of contempt against the King or the government, a joke, a detached phrase, was enough. It is incredible how many people, justly or unjustly, were more or less ruined, always without resource, without trial, and without knowing why. The secret was impenetrable; for nothing ever cost the King less than profound silence and dissimulation.

This last talent he pushed almost to falsehood, but never to deceit, pluming himself upon keeping his word,—therefore he scarcely ever gave it. The secrets of others he kept as religiously as his own. He was even flattered by certain confessions and certain confidences; and there was no mistress, minister, or favourite, who could have wormed them out, even though the secret regarded themselves.

We know, amongst many others, the famous story of a woman of quality, who, after having been separated a year from her husband, found herself in the family-way just as he was on the point of returning from the army, and who, not knowing what else to do, in the most urgent manner begged a private interview of the King. She obtained it, and confided to him her position, as to the worthiest man in his realm, as she said. The King counselled her to profit by her distress, and live more wisely for the future, and immediately promised to retain her husband on the frontier as long as was necessary, and to forbid his return under any pretext, and in fact he gave orders the same day to Louvois, and prohibited the husband not only all leave of absence, but forbade him to quit for a single day the post he was to command all the winter. The officer, who was distinguished, and who had neither wished nor asked to be employed all the winter upon the frontier, and Louvois, who had in no way thought of it, were equally surprised and vexed. They were obliged, however, to obey to the letter, and without asking why; and the King never mentioned the circumstance until many years afterwards, when he was quite sure nobody could find out either husband or wife, as in fact they never could, or even obtain the most vague or the most uncertain suspicion.

The King's *Politesse*

Never did man give with better grace than Louis XIV, or augmented so much, in this way, the price of his benefits. Never did man sell to better profit his words, even his smiles,—nay, his looks. Never did disobliging words escape him; and if he had to blame, to reprimand, or correct, which was very rare, it was nearly always with goodness, never, except on one occasion (the admonition of Courtenvaux, related in its place), with anger or severity. Never was man so naturally polite, or of a politeness so measured, so graduated, so adapted to person, time, and place. Towards women his politeness was without parallel. Never did he pass the humblest petticoat without raising his hat; even to chambermaids, that he knew to be such, as often happened at Marly. For ladies he took his hat off completely, but to a greater or less extent; for titled people, half off, holding it in his hand or against his ear some instants, more or less marked. For the nobility he contented himself by putting his hand to his hat. He took it off for the Princes of the blood, as for the ladies. If he accosted ladies he did not cover himself until he had quitted them. All this was out of doors, for in the house he was never covered. His reverences, more or less marked, but always light, were incomparable for their grace and manner; even his mode of half raising himself at supper for each lady who arrived at table. Though at last this fatigued him, yet he never ceased it; the ladies who were to sit down, however, took care not to enter after supper had commenced.

If he was made to wait for anything while dressing, it was always with patience. He was exact to the hours that he gave for all his day, with a precision clear and brief in his orders. If in the bad weather of winter, when he could not go out, he went to Madame de Maintenon's a quarter of an hour earlier than he had arranged (which seldom happened), and the captain of the guards was not on duty, he did not fail afterwards to say that it was his own fault for anticipating the hour, not that of the captain of the guards for being absent. Thus, with this regularity which he never deviated from, he was served with the utmost exactitude.

He treated his valets well, above all those of the household. It was amongst them that he felt most at ease, and that he unbosomed himself the most familiarly, especially to the chiefs. Their friendship and their aversion have often had grand results. They were unceasingly in a position to render good and bad offices: thus they recalled those powerful enfranchised slaves of the Roman emperors, to whom the senate and the great people paid court and basely truckled. These valets during Louis XIV's reign were not less courted. The ministers, even the most powerful, openly studied their caprices; and the Princes of the blood,—nay, the bastards,—not to mention people of lower grade, did the same. The majority were accordingly insolent enough; and if you could not avoid their insolence, you were forced to put up with it.

The king loved air and exercise very much, as long as he could make use of them. He had excelled in dancing, and at tennis and mall. On horseback he was admirable, even at a late age. He liked to see everything done with grace and address. To acquit yourself well or ill before him was a merit or a fault. He said that with things not necessary it was best not to meddle, unless they were done well. He was very fond of shooting, and there was not a better or more graceful shot than he. He had always in his cabinet seven or eight pointer bitches, and was fond of feeding them, to make himself known to them. He was very fond, too, of stag hunting; but in a *calèche,* since he broke his arm, while hunting at Fontainebleau, immediately after the death of the Queen. He rode alone in a species of "box," drawn by four little horses—with five or six relays, and drove himself with an address and accuracy unknown to the best coachmen. His postilions were children from ten to fifteen years of age, and he directed them.

He liked splendour, magnificence, and profusion in everything: you pleased him if you shone through the brilliancy of your houses, your clothes, your table, your equipages. Thus a taste for extravagance and luxury was disseminated through all classes of society; causing infinite harm, and leading to general confusion of rank and to ruin.

As for the King himself, nobody ever approached his magnificence. His buildings, who could number them? At the same time, who was there who did not deplore the pride, the caprice, the bad taste seen in them? He built nothing useful or ornamental in Paris, except the Pont Royal, and that simply by necessity; so that despite its incomparable extent, Paris is inferior to many cities of Europe. Saint-Germain, a lovely spot, with a marvellous view, rich forest, terraces, gardens, and water he abandoned for Versailles; the dullest and most ungrateful of all places, without prospect, without wood, without water, without soil; for the ground is all shifting sand or swamp, the air accordingly bad.

The King Creates a Palace

But he liked to subjugate nature by art and treasure. He built at Versailles, without any general design, the beautiful and the ugly, the vast and the mean, all jumbled together. His own apartments and those of the Queen, are inconvenient to the last degree, dull, close, stinking. The gardens astonish by their magnificence, but cause regret by their bad taste. You are introduced to the freshness of the shade only by a vast torrid zone, at the end of which there is nothing for you but to mount or descend; and with the hill, which is very short, terminate the gardens. The violence everywhere done to nature repels and wearies us despite ourselves. The abundance of water, forced up and gathered together from all parts, is rendered green, thick, muddy; it disseminates humidity, unhealthy and evident; and an odour still more so. I might never finish upon the monstrous defects of a palace so immense and so immensely dear, with its accompaniments, which are still more so.

But the supply of water for the fountains was all defective at all moments, in spite of those seas of reservoirs which had cost so many millions to establish and to form upon the shifting sand and marsh. Who could have believed it? This defect became the ruin of the infantry which was turned out to do the work. Madame de Maintenon reigned. M. de Louvois was well with her, then. We were at peace. He conceived the idea of turning the river Eure between Chartres and Maintenon, and of making it come to Versailles. Who can say what gold and men this obstinate attempt cost during several years, until it was prohibited by the heaviest penalties, in the camp established there, and for a long time kept up; not to speak of the sick,—above all, of the dead,—that the hard labour and still more the much disturbed earth, caused? How many men were years in recovering from the effects of the contagion! How many never regained their health at all! And not only the sub-officers, but the colonels, the brigadiers and general officers, were compelled to be upon the spot, and were not at liberty to absent themselves a quarter of an hour from the works. The war at last interrupted them in 1688, and they have never since been undertaken; only unfinished portions of them exist which immortalise this cruel folly.

THE PRUSSIAN MINISTER'S ASSESSMENT
OF LOUIS XIV'S KINGSHIP [4]

Few foreign observers were better qualified to weigh Louis XIV's qualities as a ruler and as a man than Ézéchiel Spanheim (1629–1710), who thrice served as envoy to France (1666, 1668, and 1678–87) from several German princes. During Spanheim's last embassy, which he undertook for the Elector of Brandenburg-Prussia, he drew up a description of Louis and his court from which this selection is taken. Although Spanheim follows the classical spirit of portraiture, balancing Louis's strengths against his weaknesses, his fear of the king's secret, his love of grandeur, his obstinacy, and his lust for gloire gives a negative tone to his assessment.

The Good Qualities of the King

So that one can recall again what I have just said about the good qualities of His Majesty, although he is not brilliant, or very penetrating in his judgment, or very insightful, he has however enough good qualities to fulfill the duties of a great king. He is in good health; he has taste, discrimination, and sufficient shrewdness not to let himself be taken by surprise; and he rewards merit when he finds it. Moreover, he is neither naturally sullen, nor quick-tempered, nor a scoffer, nor does he enjoy raillery at the expense of another person. This latter is a rare quality in a court and nation filled with men of this type. For one not learned or ever having devoted himself to study, or ever having been attracted by it, he writes well and correctly. He loves the fine arts and promotes them; he is particularly knowledgeable about music, painting, and building construction. He judges people and things sanely and fairly, in so far as he has some knowledge of them. He is master, as I have said before, of his *secret* [confidential knowledge of people and diplomacy] . . . ; he happily employs his *secret* as one of the principal instruments to insure the success of his undertakings. Thus, there is no second chance for

[4] From Ézéchiel Spanheim, *Relation de France en 1690*, ed. Charles Schefer (Paris: Renouard, 1883), pp. 4–9. Translated by John C. Rule.

those whom he has honored with his affection, and who, through indiscretion or weakness, betray his confidence. It is through his *secret* that he holds the fickle and indiscreet moods of the courtiers, and impresses with restraint and cautiousness those who through their office or through friendship with the king, are around him the most. Therefore, he speaks little but at the right moment; he expresses himself correctly and with dignity. He has complete self-control in parades and audiences in order to keep himself within his self-prescribed limits, so as not to extend himself beyond those limits and so that he does nothing which would be wrong or which would expose himself. This is what I have noticed, among other things, in so many of the private and public audiences, during not only my two embassies to France in the service of the late Elector Palatine, Charles-Louis, in 1666 and 1668, and which were of short duration, but particularly in my last employment and sojourn of nine years in the service of the late His Highness the Elector and of His Highness the reigning Elector. One can add that, fortunately, he knows how to maintain a delicate admixture of grandeur and intimacy in his private conversations and knows how to conduct himself without either arrogance or ignobleness.

His inclinations are naturally directed to uprightness, justice and equity, when they are not diverted . . . by bad advice or by motives of interest, *gloire*, or, in a word, by the desire for the grandeur of his reign. He enjoys doing good by choice or impulse; sometimes he does favors like a friend, as he has done in regard to some of his favorites, other times as a lover, but most often as a master. In addition, the disorder in which he found the finances at the time of Cardinal Mazarin's death instilled in him a strong inclination for saving money and for not being extravagant, except for expenditures in such things as buildings or for promises of honor or passion given to secret agents or mistresses. Since he likes order, . . . and moderation, and since he is faithful to the duties of his religion and practices them very regularly, he has, as a result, a well-regulated court and submissive courtiers. He knows how to steer his court from vices which were only too frequently committed—quarrels, debauchery, impiety, profligacy, and the irreverent worship of God. He has also openly pronounced against the flagrant vices of the youth of the court and the disgraceful conduct of his own children, and he does not fail to punish or correct those who are suspected of misbehavior, such as the Duc de Vermandois, son of the king and Madame de la Vallière, and the Prince de Conti, one of the princes of the blood. This, thus, is proof that the king is by nature the enemy of vice, except for those times, perhaps, when he is carried away by his temperament and by bad examples (which will be discussed later); that he is, moreover, moderate in his passions, master of his conduct and not inclined to anger and rage. His conduct is as regular and uniform in amusements as in government affairs; thus, he does not dissipate or demean himself in the former or become lax in the latter. He did not display any less resoluteness of soul during the times when he was in the grips of a distressing illness and when painful remedies were used to cure him.

The Bad Qualities of the King

But among these good and attractive qualities of the king, which have brought and do bring much brilliance and advantage to him and to the fortunate successes of his reign, there are other traits which are not so advantageous to him. In the first place, he has an intelligence that is naturally rather limited, which was improved very little, as I said before, in his youth, by those who wished to keep him out of government affairs. He has only improved upon this mediocrity [of mind], which birth had given him and which an education has left untouched, by the changes which he has made in the government, and by the order he has brought out of disorder after Cardinal Mazarin's death, and since then by the long and fortunate success of his reign. He has made an art of ruling, not so much by knowledge or by reflexion as by circumstances and habit, so that one can say, without offending that the king, and in spite of the exaggerated adulations of his eulogists, is not one of those geniuses of the first rank who sees, who penetrates, who decides, who undertakes everything by himself, and who formulates the plan and executes the project. . . . From this also stems the king's rather limited capacity in comprehending the basis of governmental affairs, which makes him easily engrossed with people in whom he has confidence and in whom he believes are in no way informed about such matters. He also has an attachment, or, more precisely, an obstinacy, which is not any less great, for executing plans or projects formulated or recommended by a persuasive or cunning minister. One can also add the king evinces jealousy, or true but masked aversion, for anyone who competes with his grandeur, power, and attainments, or is the object of esteem or public veneration. Thus, he directs his plans and operations more often by the force of his authority and by convenience than by honesty and justice. In fact, he judges government affairs and public interests less in their own light than by what others judge them to be. The idea of his grandeur . . . preoccupies him, and he reflects more on the past successes of his reign than on the pretexts and means used to achieve them or indeed on the fortunate circumstances which played an important part in shaping them. After all, even if he had enough talent to understand the great issues, he does not concern himself enough with them to direct them or to envisage them in all of their aspects. The great diligence which he displays in the councils is limited mostly to giving precedence to reports which are prepared for him in advance, to the resolutions which conform to his opinions and which are enacted in his presence, and to the choice of the methods or the people to insure their success. Jealous in every way of his authority, sensitive otherwise to all that concerns it, or could endanger it, he is easily swayed to endorse the advice given to him and the measures proposed to sustain it . . . This is the fatal source of the calamities and wars which surprised and afflicted Europe several times and which ravage it today. Moreover, as he is more inclined to have his subjects regard him as a master than as a father, his reward is their submission and dependence rather than their affection. He is not motivated by a real desire to relieve them their miseries. Thus, it can be said, if he loves to give, he loves more to save; that his kindness or generosity is ordinarily motivated by self-interest; that he gives even as much or more by ostentation as by choice. Therefore, he is the friend both of splendor and of economy. Often, there is extravagance where there could be thrift and too much thrift where a little more expense would be better. One needs only reflect, on the one hand, upon the twenty-four millions that the château, the gardens, and the fountains of Versailles cost,[5] or on the work begun on Madame de Maintenon's aqueduct, where more than thirty thousand men worked for

[5] In terms of today's buying power the palace of Versailles probably cost between 180 and 200 million dollars and this would be a conservative estimate.

three years to direct, for a distance of sixteen leagues, the water of a river into the reservoirs of Versailles. On the other hand, one need only reflect on the misery of the common people and the peasants, exhausted by the *tailles*,[6] by having to lodge soldiers, by the *gabelles*,[7] and, finally, on the little care the king has taken to treat his friends and allies kindly and to fulfill the obligations he should undertake on their behalf.

[6] The direct government tax levied on income or land of the members of the Third Estate.

[7] Tax on commodities, the most famous being on salt.

5
Louis XIV at Home

These sketches of Louis XIV's home life were
written by Françoise d'Aubigné, Marquise of Maintenon
(1635–1719), the king's second wife, and by the Duke of
Saint-Simon. Louis's morganatic[1] marriage to Maintenon
(probably in 1684) helped give stability to his personal life.
When he wearied of court ceremony Louis retreated to
Maintenon's rooms, where he could confide in her his secret
worries and gnawing fears. Maintenon played the role of
confidante with consummate skill: she was an excellent
listener, who wielded considerable influence in family affairs, on religious appointments, and, at times, on politics.
Maintenon influenced political decisions through her friends
in the ministry, Michel Chamillart and Daniel-François
Voysin, and through Louis's confessor, Father Le Tellier.
On occasion, as Colbert de Torcy testifies (Chapter 6) she
intervened directly in affairs. She used extreme caution,
however, in giving advice to Louis because she knew that
he disliked "meddling females," and as she told the Princess
des Ursins, "I am not regularly consulted." Her daily life
was usually crowded not by matters of statecraft but by the
mundane comings and goings of the king's family, secretaries, petitioners, and friends. We can note with sympathy
her cry: "I hurry, I hurry . . ."

The selection from Saint-Simon portrays Louis as a self-
absorbed, callous, domestic tyrant.

[1] A marriage by which the wife and any children of the marriage have
no legal claim on or to the crown.

MME DE MAINTENON TO THE PRINCESS DES URSINS [2]

Saint Cyr, May 8th, 1707

It is very just to thank the God of battles for that which he has enabled us to gain, and you have so well conceived the joy of the King and that of all the royal family, that I cannot refrain from communicating to you the particulars. You know Marly, and my apartment; the King was alone in my little room, and I was sitting down to table in my closet, through which it was necessary to pass; an officer of the guards cried out at the door, "Here is M. de Chamillart." The King answered, "What! he himself?" because he was not expected to come; I threw down my napkin, with emotion, on which M. de Chamillart said, "That's right!" and entered immediately, followed by M. de Silly, whom I did not know: you may well imagine that I also entered. I then heard of the defeat of the enemy's army, and returned to sup in very good humour. The Dauphin, who was playing, or looking on in the saloon, soon joined the King, and the Duke of Burgundy entered with a billiard mace in his hand; Madame, to whom a message had been dispatched with the news that the Duke of Orleans had gained a battle, arrived soon after. I told her that he was not there, at which she was very angry, and I understood that she said, "I shall soon hear that my son has hanged himself." Madame de Dangeau left the table to go and write to her husband who was at Paris. I reperuse with pleasure those parts of your letter of the 17th April, in which you tell me of the advantages that would follow the winning of a battle in Spain. God grant that you may prove a true prophetess!

MME DE MAINTENON TO THE PRINCESS DES URSINS [3]

Saint Cyr, November 25th, 1708

. . .

I had no occasion for the memorial which you have sent me

[2] From *The Secret Correspondence of Madame de Maintenon, with the Princess des Ursins;* from the Original Manuscripts in the possession of the Duke de Choiseul (London: Geo. B. Whittaker, 1827), pp. 100–102, 204–5, 213–14, 370–71.

[3] *Ibid.*

about the Duke of Orleans; I know your uprightness, and that of all those with whom he has been in communication, too well to have doubted a moment of his being in the wrong, had he complained of them. I shall, however, keep this memoir and show it to the King, in case any thing should be published on the subject; it would not become me to let it be seen by any one else, and even the King himself shall not see it without your consent. I know, better than any other person, how much you esteem and praise the Duke; but our Princes have such a disposition to believe whatever their domestics say, that it is quite insufferable, and often puts me out of patience: their own truth and sincerity cannot be too much esteemed, but these qualities sometimes are injurious to them, by preventing them from perceiving that others are not the same as themselves.

The King partakes of this truth and sincerity, and as the head of the royal family he never thought of deceiving his grandson: it is true that he does not think peace so near as our generals imagine; but it is equally so that the King knows the absolute necessity of it, which you would also be convinced of were you here.

MME DE MAINTENON TO THE PRINCESS DES URSINS [4]

Versailles, December 23rd, 1708

You know I dare say by this time, that the end of the campaign had been truly pitiful, and that the enemy has already the audacity to besiege Ghent, hoping that it will have as fortunate a result as the siege of Lille. The defence of Marshal de Boufflers has shown us how rash this enterprise was, since he gave an opportunity to our army for four months to succour him, during which time we only made one feeble attempt, that of the Chevalier de Luxembourg, which succeeded; one upon a greater scale would have had the same success, and more important results.

You are right in saying that we ought to behold the hand of Providence in all this: our King was too glorious; God wishes to humble in order to save him; France had aggrandized herself too much, perhaps unjustly; he wishes to confine her within narrower limits, and which will be, no doubt, more substantial.

[4] *Ibid.*

Our nation was insolent and dissolute; it has pleased the Almighty to punish and abase it. It is only your concerns which I do not see in so clear a light: a virtuous King's [Philip V] rights founded on justice; a Prince called for by all his people declared heir to the crown by his predecessor on the bed of death, against all his natural inclinations: a Queen [of Spain] who is the honour of her sex, and of the Princesses of her rank; a marriage formed by a conformity of sentiments as to greatness, goodness, and justice, and blest with a successor, who holds out the most flattering hopes:—that all this should be contrary to the order and will of God is what I do not comprehend, and which he alone will one day clear up.

MME DE MAINTENON TO THE PRINCESS DES URSINS [5]

Versailles, March 17th, 1712

The Duchess of Alba brought me your letter yesterday, and handed it to me very secretly, when my room was very full of company: I could not peruse it without shedding many tears, as I easily conceive the grief of their Majesties at the loss of the Dauphin.[6] They know by this time of a third loss, which they will feel less sensibly, but which is still of great consequence. You cannot imagine the state of the court, nor is there less sorrow at present than there was a month ago. Poor Madame de Ventadour[7] is inconsolable, and to complete her affliction, she hears it insinuated that it would be desirable for the child which remains to us to share the same fate as his brother.

I was yesterday evening on the point of telling the King what has passed in your mind respecting Cardinal Gualterio;[8] but, after much reflection, I thought it would be better not to mention it; the King would have communicated it to his ministers, who would have been displeased with you, and perhaps have published it; nor would our great lords have been obliged to you; and I do not wish you to be feared. As to the affair itself, it appeared to me that Cardinals could not be approved of in a council of Regency, and I think there would be still greater repugnance to admitting a foreigner; in other respects, he whom

---

[5] *Ibid.*
[6] Louis, Duke of Burgundy.
[7] Governess to Louis XV.
[8] Former nuncio to France.

you propose is highly esteemed, and a favourite with the King and the whole court. His Majesty appears to be extremely well satisfied with Cardinal de la Trémoïlle;[9] but in whatever way things may turn out, I conjure you to look upon me as a woman incapable of managing public affairs, and who has heard them talked of too late in life to possess any talents in such matters,—but, above all, one who hates them still more on account of her ignorance. I am not regularly consulted, and can assure you that my influence diminishes daily. I am now seventy-five years old, and it appears to me that I have only to prepare for death. You will, therefore, not be astonished that my ideas are a little serious. If I have formed an incorrect judgment of Cardinal Gualterio, there will always be time to retract.

MME DE MAINTENON'S DESCRIPTION OF HER LIFE AT COURT MADE AT SAINT-CYR TO MME DE GLAPION [10]

Ca. 1705

. . . "This is true," replied Madame [de Maintenon]. "I have told you often that the only time I can take for my prayers and the mass is when other people sleep; without it, I could not go on; for when people once begin to enter my room I am not my own mistress; I have not an instant to myself." I [Mme de Glapion] replied, as to that, that I always imagined her room to be like the shop of a great merchant, which, once opened, is never empty and where the shopman must remain. "That is just how it is," said Madame. "They begin to come in about half-past seven; first it is M. Maréchal [the king's surgeon]; he has no sooner gone than M. Fagon [king's doctor] enters; he is followed by M. Bloin [the king's head valet] or some one else sent to inquire how I am. Sometimes I have extremely pressing letters to write, which I must get in here. Next come persons of greater consequence: one day, M. Chamillart; another, the archbishop; to-day, a general of the army on the point of departure; to-morrow, an audience that I must give, having been demanded under such circumstances that I cannot defer it. M. le Duc du Maine waited the other day in my antechamber till M. Chamil-

[9] Mme. des Ursins's brother, ambassador in Rome.
[10] From *The Correspondence of Madame Princess Palatine, Marie-Adelaide de Savoie, and of Madame de Maintenon.* Trans. Katharine Prescott Wormeley (Boston: Hardy, Pratt & Co., 1902).

lart had finished. When M. Chamillart went out M. du Maine came in and kept me till the king arrived; for there is a little etiquette in this, that no one leaves me till some one of higher rank enters and sends them away. When the king comes, they all have to go. The king stays till he goes to mass. I do not know if you have observed that all this time I am not yet dressed; if I were I should not have been able to say my prayers. I still have my night-cap on; but my room by this time is like a church; a perpetual procession is going on, everybody passes through it; the comings and goings are endless.

"When the king has heard mass he returns to me; next comes the Duchess of Burgundy with a number of ladies, and there they stay while I eat my dinner. You would think that here at least was a time I could have to myself; but you shall see how it is. I fret lest the Duchess of Burgundy should do something unsuitable; I try to make her say a word to this one; I look to see if she treats that one properly, and whether she is behaving well to her husband. I must entertain the company, and do it in a way to unite them all. If some one commits an indiscretion I feel it; I am worried by the manner in which people take what is said to them; in short, it is a tumult of mind that nothing equals. Around me stand a circle of ladies, so that I cannot even ask for something to drink. . . .

"After the king's dinner is over, he comes with all the princesses and the royal family into my room; and they cause it to be intolerably hot. They talk; the king stays about half an hour; then he goes away, but no one else; the rest remain . . . they surround me, and I am forced to listen to the jokes of Mme. la Maréchale de Clérembault, the satire of this one, and the tales of that one. They have nothing to do, those good ladies; and they have done nothing all the morning. It is not so with me, who have much else to do than to sit there and talk, probably with a heart full of care, grief, and distress at bad news, like that from Verrue lately. I have everything on my mind; I am thinking how a thousand men may be perishing, and others in agony. . . . After they have all stayed some time they begin to go away, and then what do you suppose happens? One or other of these ladies invariably stays behind, wishing to speak to me in private. She takes me by the hand, leads me into my little room and tells me frequently the most unpleasant and wearisome things, for, as you may well suppose, it is not my affairs that they talk about; they are those of their own family: one has had a quarrel with her husband; another wants to obtain something from the king; an ill turn has been done to this one; a false report has been spread about that one; domestic troubles have embroiled a third; and I am forced to listen to all this, and the one among them whom I like least does not restrain herself more than the others,—she tells me everything; I must be told all the circumstances and speak about them to the king. Often the Duchess of Burgundy wants to speak to me in private, like the rest.

"When the king returns from hunting he comes to me; then my door is closed and no one enters. Here I am, then, alone with him. I must bear his troubles, if he has any, his sadness, his nervous dejection; sometimes he bursts into tears which he cannot control, or else he complains of illness. He has no conversation. Then a minister comes, who often brings fatal news; the king works. If they wish me to be a third in their consultation, they call me; if they do not want me I retire to a little distance, and it is then that I sometimes make my afternoon prayers; I pray to God for about half an hour. If they wish me to hear what is said I cannot do this; I sit there, and hear perhaps that things are going ill; a courier has arrived with bad news; and all that wrings my heart and prevents me from sleeping at night.

"While the king continues to work I sup; but it is not once in two months that I can do so at my ease. I feel that the king is alone, or I have left him sad, or that M. Chamillart has almost finished with him; sometimes he sends and begs me to make haste. Another day he wants to show me something. So that I am always hurried, and the only thing I can do is to eat very fast. I have my fruit brought with the meat to hasten supper; and all this as fast as I can. I leave Mme. d'Heudicourt and Mme. de Dangeau at table, because they cannot eat as fast as I do, and often I am oppressed by it.

"After this it is, as you may suppose, getting late. I have been about since six in the morning; I have not breathed freely the whole day; I am overcome with weariness and yawning; more than that, I begin to feel what it is that makes old age; I find myself at last so weary that I can no more. Sometimes the king perceives it and says: 'You are very tired, are you not? You ought to go to bed.' So I go to bed; my women come and undress me; but I feel that the king wants to talk to me and is waiting till they go; or some minister still remains and he fears my women will hear what he says. That makes him uneasy, and me too. What can I do? I hurry; I hurry so that I almost faint; and you must know that all my life what I have hated most is to be hurried. At five years of age it had the same effect upon me; I was faint if I ran too fast, for being naturally very quick and consequently inclined to haste, I was also very delicate, so that to run, as I tell you, choked me. Well, at last I am in bed; I send away my women; the king approaches and sits down by my pillow. What can I do then? I am in bed, but I have need of many things; mine is not a glorified body without wants. There is no one there whom I can ask for what I need; not a single woman. It is not because I could not have them, for the king is full of kindness, and if he thought I wanted one woman he would endure ten; but it never comes into his mind that I am constraining myself. As he is master everywhere, and does exactly what he wishes, he cannot imagine that any one should do otherwise; he believes that if I show no wants, I have none. You know that my rule is to take everything on myself and think for others. Great people, as a rule, are not like that; they never constrain themselves, they never think that others are constrained by them, nor do they feel grateful for it, simply because they are so accustomed to see everything done in reference only to themselves that they are no longer struck by it and pay no heed. I have sometimes, during my severe colds, been on the point of choking with a cough I was unable to check. M. de Pontchartrain, who saw me one day all crimson with the effort, said to the king: 'She cannot bear it; some one must be called.'

"The king stays with me till he goes to supper, and about a quarter of an hour before the supper is served M. le Dauphin, M. le Duc and Mme. la Duchess de Burgundy come to me. At ten o'clock or a quarter past ten everybody goes away. There is my day. I am now alone, and I take the relief of which I am in need; but often the anxieties and fatigues I have gone through keep me from sleeping."

LOUIS XIV'S DOMESTIC TYRANNY [11]

Of all his loves Louis XIV never really loved anyone but himself. His mistresses, whether ill, or pregnant, or still recovering from childbirth, were forced to attend festivals and meals in full evening dress, to eat and chatter gaily as if they were in the best of health. They were also made to travel when they were in the same condition. Louis was no kinder to Madame de Maintenon. I saw her go to Fontainebleau, she with a high fever and an unbearable headache, at a time when it was wagered that she would not arrive there alive. He opened all the drapes and windows, and lit the candles, sparing her no inconveniences, [even having] the musicians perform in the same room in which Mme de Maintenon was resting. He was just as inconsiderate of his own family. He dragged the Duchess of Berry, pregnant for the first time, and with a fever, to Fontainebleau, despite the warnings of the physicians and of Mme de Maintenon. The princess injured herself and had a miscarriage the day after their arrival. He did the same to the Duchess of Burgundy, who . . . was the only member of his family whom he really loved. She was pregnant and ill but he refused to postpone a trip to Marly; nor would he permit her to remain at Versailles, despite the protests that were made to him because she had not borne any other children before this time. A few days after her arrival at Marly she injured herself and miscarried. The Duchess de Lude came to inform the King of it in his gardens. He was amusing himself watching a pond of carps and I was present. We saw the Duchess de Lude enter. Upon seeing her Louis exclaimed, "God be thanked! the Duchess of Burgundy is in labor!" "Why give thanks to God?" replied the Duc de la Rochefoucauld, "you haven't any grandchildren and what could be a worse misfortune in the world than a miscarriage. And often after such miscarriages a woman can not bear any more children." "Eh, what does it matter whether I acquire children by the Duke of

[11] From *Écrits inédits de Saint-Simon*, ed. M. P. Faugère, 8 vols. (Paris: Plon et Cie, 1880–93), Vol. I (1880), pp. 82–84. Translated by John C. Rule.

Burgundy or the Duke of Berry? At least I'll be free to rest and go where I please without women and doctors trailing behind me with their protests." All who were present were overwhelmed by these words. It was more than a quarter of an hour later before anyone spoke a word. The King then continued his walk.

His family did not receive any more consideration than anyone else. They were the slaves to his schedule. He conducted himself as a king in front of them just as much as he did before his court and demanded of them the same constant attentiveness. No one ever saw him mourn for anyone. Even those closest to him he mourned only briefly and with restraint. He did not understand how others could be so grieved over the deaths of their loved ones . . . ; he was downright relieved by the deaths of his ministers and great generals, even to the point of showing his relief in public. The authority and prestige that the first ministers and generals had, troubled him; only in the company of his mistresses and valets did he feel at ease.

6

The King at Work

In the four selections that follow, a careful analysis is made of Louis XIV's working habits: of his attitude toward his ministers, theirs toward him, and of the manner in which he presided over France's elaborate conciliar form of government. The first and most general account is given by the Duke of Saint-Simon, who believes that the king's ministers usurped power from the "original lieutenants of the realm"—the greater nobility—and that "by degrees" these ambitious men arrogated to themselves "favor and fortune." The third selection, by the able political pamphleteer Charles Irénée Castel, Abbé de Saint-Pierre (1658–1743), points up the fact that the king governed both through his councils and through the individual ministers. Indeed, the latter had gained so much power that by 1702 Saint-Pierre reports that the "King knows of the affairs of his marine ministry nearly exclusively through his minister." Hugues de Lionne (1611–71), Louis's foreign minister in the 1660's, comments on the king's passion for detail; and Jean-Baptiste Colbert de Torcy (1665–1746), foreign minister from 1696–1715, shows, in the selection taken from his Journal, that though the king remained an indefatigable worker, he had by 1710 turned into a crotchety, insufferable old bore, increasingly given to temper tantrums and to tears. Torcy's description of the king's blotched face and his querulous voice serve as a striking contrast to Lionne's account of the confident, eager young man of the 1660's.

C'EST LA FAUTE AUX MINISTRES [1]

One of the ministers left in office at the time of Cardinal Mazarin's death was [Nicholas] Fouquet, superintendant of finances. On his deathbed Mazarin advised the king and the queen

[1] From *Écrits inédits de Saint-Simon*, ed. M. P. Faugère, 8 vols. (Paris: Plon et Cie, 1880), Vol. I, pp. 215–18. Translated by John C. Rule.

mother to dismiss Fouquet in favor of Colbert, who was the
most skilled servant Mazarin had ever employed in matters of
finance and business . . . [and] was the intendant of the cardinal's household and . . . one of the last intendants of finances.
[Louis XIV] . . . did not delay in following Mazarin's advice;
and though Colbert never dared call himself superintendant he
actually assumed the powers of the office; indeed in the name of
the controller-general Colbert signed everything for the king,
while persuading Louis XIV that the king managed his own
finances. . . . Soon after this Colbert also obtained the post of
Secretary of State for the Department of the Marine. . . .[2] The
other ministers left in office were [Michel] Le Tellier, Secretary
of State for War, and [Hugues] de Lionne [as minister of foreign
affairs], who died in 1671 and was replaced by [Arnauld de]
Pomponne. Shortly before Lionne's death Louvois received his
right of inheritance to his father's secretaryship; the elder Le
Tellier became chancellor in 1677. By that time Louvois was
already strongly established in office and worked under his father's constant supervision [until 1677].

These strong men understood very well the king's nature:
Louis XIV, they observed, displayed some natural intelligence
combined with straightforward common sense, an incredible
general ignorance, a general distrust of everyone and everything,
and a thirst for grandeur, for complete mastery over men, and
for *gloire*. They recognized also Louis's fear of being governed
(to the point of parading the fact that he was not); his kindness
and natural poise; his passion for complete control of everything. . . . These ministers of Louis XIV, while working hard
for the good of the state, did not fail to profit from their knowledge of the king's character. They ingrained in Louis a desire
for grandeur . . . in order to exercise authority themselves;
they reduced men around them to complete dependence, elevat-
ing themselves to a position equal to the greatest at court. At
the same time they persuaded the king that any infringement of
their authority was a usurpation of his own; thus they fused their
authority with his. By degrees, then, they have elevated themselves to their present pinnacle of power. In order to remove
any mistrust of their authority and at the same time reassure
him that he truly did govern, the ministers overwhelmed Louis

[2] Actually in 1669.

with details of government. True to character, Louis became avidly absorbed in such details, while becoming increasingly convinced that he alone governed. In truth a vast number of the more important matters remained in the ministers' hands; thus by dazzling the king with petty details, they masked their own activities and sidetracked the king without his realizing it. But even after these precautions had been taken they did not feel secure. The king's goodness and natural poise upset them; and even more upsetting was the access favorite courtiers had to the king; these same courtiers might betray them by informing the king of their maneuvers. They made it appear then that such free access to the king was not only beneath but an attack on his dignity. . . . Moreover, they made it appear that the king's private life would be constantly disturbed by a thousand captious and dangerous appeals or by matters that the courtiers knew nothing about since the ministers alone had accurate information of matters of state, and they alone knew the origin, progress, and scope of affairs. Consequently, all governmental business, they argued, should be directed to the individual minister in his own department.

Thus by surrounding the king with almost Asiatic grandeur, they succeeded in isolating Louis XIV, so one could meet him only in public and [if one wanted a private interview] men of all stations—great and small alike—had to clear the matter with the ministers. In this way they became absolute masters of all state affairs, of favors, and fortunes; little by little they arrogated power to themselves and when Louis did escape their surveillance it was by indirect means; such occasions, moreover, were rare and not significant. . . .

THE KING'S COMING OF AGE[3]

Those who believed that our master would soon ignore government affairs were indeed mistaken, since as the years pass, the more he takes pleasure in applying himself to the work and devoting himself completely to it. You will find very convincing proof of it in the enclosed dispatch addressed to you, in which

[3] Lionne to d'Éstrades, August 5, 1661, describing Louis XIV at work. From J. J. Jusserand, *A French Ambassador at the Court of Charles the Second* (New York: G. P. Putnam's Sons; London: T. Fisher Unwin, 1892), pp. 188–89. Translated by J. C. Rule.

you will see the resolution that His Majesty has taken to reply personally to all ambassadors' letters concerning the most important and secret affairs. It's an idea which came to him of his own accord, as you can imagine that no one would have been bold enough to dare to suggest that he impose such a great amount of work on himself. This is how great kings are made, and, since France has been a monarchy, I do not know when there has been any king who wanted to take on such a great amount of work, or more useful work, whether for the king himself or for the well-being and glory of his subjects and his State.

He works in this manner: I have the honor to read to him the most secret dispatches, after they have been decoded, addressed to him at my office. Next, he honors me by informing me of his proposed response, which I compose point by point in his presence. His Majesty corrects me when I do not precisely express his thoughts. Without flattery or exaggeration, I assure you that I am learning more than I ever thought myself capable of learning. After finishing the dispatch, I am careful to have copies of it made. Then I have the honor of presenting it to him to sign, which he does with his own hand and not with a printed signature, as is customary in the offices of the secretaries of state.

FROM A LETTER BY ABBÉ DE SAINT-PIERRE [4]

July 3, 1702

There are three councils that the king attends. The Council of Ministers[5] usually meets on Sundays, Mondays, Wednesdays, and Thursdays when the court is not at Marly and almost always in the morning at about a quarter to ten when the king returns from mass until about one o'clock when the king sits down to eat his midday meal. Usually monseigneur the dauphin [attends these sessions], and always the chancellor [M. de Ponchartrain], M. de Beauvilliers, M. de Torcy, and M. de Chamillart, the latter the minister of finance and war, attend this meeting. The Duke of Burgundy does not attend yet, nor do the secretaries of state who are not ministers.

M. de Torcy, secretary of state for the department of foreign

[4] From "The Councils of Louis XIV," ed. Merle L. Perkins, *French Review*, Volume 30, No. 5, April 1957, pp. 395–97; trans. J. C. Rule. Reproduced in English translation by permission of the publisher.
[5] *Conseil d'en haut.*

affairs, gives a report solely on foreign affairs. He reads the letters that he has recently decoded and advises the council on the best way in which to answer them. Then, if the business is of a routine nature and if the king is of the same opinion as M. de Torcy, Louis XIV says it seems good to him; if not, and if the business is very important, he seeks the advice of his council. Monseigneur the dauphin gives his opinion at once; the council members, following Torcy's example, read over the letters that Torcy has recently written and the responses that have been made to the French ambassadors in order to learn if what has been written conforms to the resolution taken in the last council meeting; Torcy records responses in order to have them for reference for the next meeting.

The ministers are not given official letters of appointment as ministers; their commission is given verbally. The pensions, or ministers' salaries, are twenty thousand francs a year.

The Council of Finances meets Tuesday and Saturday mornings after mass until the midday meal, that is about 2:30 to 2:45 in the afternoon. The business [discussed there] concerns difficulties which are found in the execution of edicts involving money, the contracts with the tax-farmers, leases with various companies, disagreements between tax-farmers and various companies, also various schemes for raising extraordinary taxes during wartime. . . . The session of the Council of Finance is like that of the Council of Ministers: the king sits at the head of a long table.

The Council of Dispatches usually meets every two weeks on Monday mornings; then on that day the Council of Ministers does not meet . . . ; sometimes the king meets this council in the late afternoon when he has taken his medicine and cannot go out. The Duke of Burgundy enters and sits opposite his father, the Dauphin; but when the Dauphin is not present the Duke of Burgundy sits in his place. Matters reviewed by this council concern quarrels between garrison officers for precedence or for rights between army officers and the civil judges, between parlements and other superior courts. In this meeting the king counts the votes and decides by majority rule, sometimes deciding against his own opinion. It is a question of insuring fairness between friend and foe, and he thinks of himself as only the presiding officer.

The Council of Religion[6] meets only once a month, on Saturday after the king has dined. It should be more properly called
a Council of Dispatches *extraordinaire* at which the four secretaries of state report what is happening in their departments as
regards Protestants or new converts, annuities, management of
the possessions of those Protestants who have fled the country, as
well as matters concerning bishops and clergy.

Such are the councils, such is the public work of the king; but
he also works on Friday mornings alone with his confessor, the
Jesuit Père de la Chaise, on the administration of convents,
matters concerning clergymen whose moral conduct has been
questioned or who disagree with the teachings of the church;
however, most of his time is occupied with the distribution of
bishoprics, of superior posts in the monasteries, of pensions for
livings, priories, or monasteries, or other small benefices that
are granted by the king; this work lasts until supper.

Rarely are councils held after the midday meal. At that time,
if the king does not have an appointment with his doctor . . .
he takes a break at 2:30, sometimes going to the Trianon, sometimes to Marly where he oversees the workmen; more often he
goes to shoot partridges and pheasants. . . .

When he is at Marly or at Fontainebleau he hunts deer, riding
in an open carriage. Sometimes in the summer he goes in hunting
dress to stalk wild boars in [the forests of] Fontainebleau, returning about 7:30 P.M. In the winter, usually around 5:00, he changes
from his riding or hunting habit and goes to visit Mme de Maintenon. He works in her rooms with M. de Chamillart in particular on matters of finance and war, setting aside time on Sundays
to discuss financial matters, and Wednesdays and Saturdays for
war. At that time M. de Chamillart reads letters from Louis's
generals and reviews their requests. The king decides which
soldiers are to receive promotions. It is then that officers are
commissioned, sometimes generals, sometimes subordinates. The
king decides on what campaigns will be undertaken, on en-
campments, on the position of major detachments, on sieges and
battles. In regard to finances, he looks over the actual amount of
money that is in the royal treasury, the most pressing bills to be
paid; he looks at the coming monthly revenues, and what must
be distributed to the army and to the navy. The work days for

---

[6] Council of Conscience.

the secretary of state of the department of the marine are in evenings on Tuesdays and Fridays at Mme de Maintenon's apartment. He reads letters from various ports, and orders from squadron commanders. The king orders what ship construction is to be carried out, what armaments undertaken and at the same time what promotions are to be recommended. The king determines how many chiefs of squadrons, captains, and lieutenants are needed, and then decides, almost entirely on the secretary of state's report, what pensions and gratifications are to be made and what chief officers . . . [are to be advanced in rank]. Since the king knows of the affairs of his marine ministry nearly exclusively through his minister, the minister almost completely determines what advancements are to be made.

Mme de Maintenon is present near the table where the secretaries of state work. She has a piece of embroidery in her hand; she listens but rarely comments on what is being said. It is in her apartment that the king makes what preparations are needed for war; it is there he gives the orders for carrying out war measures and thus there must be great secrecy about his plans.

The Duchess of Burgundy waits in a large antechamber, where she amuses herself with her ladies. The Duke of Berry often joins them, and the Duke of Burgundy whenever he is at court. They play various card games—berlan, ombre, dupe. Once in a while the king enters the room in order to relax from his work, or when his work with the ministers is over, or when it is late, or when he has remained to chat with Mme de Maintenon. She has a light supper in the king's presence, and at 10:30, when his servants come to tell the king that his supper is ready, Louis XIV goes out and then his work is finished for another day. . . .

THE KING DISPLAYS HIS DISPLEASURE TO COLBERT DE TORCY [7]

17 December 1709

When I had finished [reading the dispatches to Louis XIV], His Majesty, sorrow quite evidently distorting his face, told me that he was extremely upset by two things I had done . . . though both had been done in good faith. I begged him to tell me how I had failed him.

[7] *Journal Inédit de Jean-Baptiste Colbert, Marquis de Torcy*, ed. Frédéric Masson (Paris: E. Plon, Nourrit et Cie, 1884), pp. 68–70; trans. J. C. Rule.

The first mistake, he said, was to have abandoned [the sea port] of Dunkirk [to the Allies]. I replied that [I had] an express order for Dunkirk's cession . . . [and] that I had reread [my orders] during the negotiations. I then assured him that if I had failed His Majesty on that article my failure was due more to overzealousness than to hasty judgment. Further [I said] peace could not be restored until the English and the Dutch received the frontiers they had demanded. Indeed the two nations had resolved not to break their alliance without first achieving the satisfaction they believed was their due because of their superiority [on the battlefield] and because of the quite apparent weakness of France. Thus I could tempt them . . . to moderate their demands only by making it evident that I had sacrificed my interests in order to satisfy theirs. In fact Prince Eugene told me one day while at the Grand Pensionary's home [at The Hague in May, 1709] that by giving the English and the Dutch everything they asked for I clearly wished to force the English and the Dutch to serve as mediators between France and the Empire; finally, if I had succeeded [in breaking up the Allied alliance] I felt I would have served the king very well indeed.

However, whatever the cause for His Majesty's renewed interest in the surrender of Dunkirk it was apparent that I had not persuaded him, even though I had had the temerity to mention the sad state of [France's] affairs as they stood in May [1709]. His Majesty still believed that too many concessions had been offered [the Allies] in the name of Peace.

I then asked him what the second mistake was: he told me that it was the abandonment of Alsace. I replied that it was precisely that charge that I was not guilty of; in fact it was because the enemy had insisted on destroying the fortresses in Alsace that I had balked at this demand as well as on the demand of the surrender of Exiles and of Fénestrelles asked for on the Duke of Savoy's behalf. I had made it clear to the Allies that I did not have the power to grant such concessions. . . .

Moreover [I reminded His Majesty] that it had been during the interval of my trip [to The Hague in May–June 1709] that His Majesty had relaxed his stand on these two conditions; that His Majesty had sent his orders to President Rouillé, who had remained at The Hague [for a time] after my departure, and that those dispatches addressed to Rouillé had been delivered to me when I arrived at Péronne on my way back to Versailles.

[In reply] the king moaned aloud that it was because his ministers were overzealous that he relaxed his usual vigilance and had followed their advice; that he very greatly regretted having continued negotiations on the conditions set down in the Preliminary Articles [of The Hague]. I said that such a concern should be the least of his worries; that I had always maintained, as had his enemies, that any one of or all of the articles could be annulled even if they were accepted at the conferences, and thus that His Majesty was pledged only to honor the last response [made] . . . and that we could immediately write to the Allies . . . that His Majesty was not bound by the conditions he had been willing to accept [the year before], and that he [now] revoked them all. But [I added] I only wished that it was as easy to support the war as it was to break off all negotiations; and that seeing the difficulties of waging a campaign [in Flanders], the plan for the invasion of Scotland seemed to me the only means [for ending the war] that was still feasible, provided, of course, that it was undertaken with the necessary military forces to make it succeed.

The king seemed to me that day extraordinarily discouraged [to the point of being] overcome by the cares of state. His misery sparked a distrust of his ministers and he attributed the failure [to come to terms with the Allies] to his ministers' weakness. . . .

Madame de Maintenon had said the evening before to M. Desmaretz [the controller-general of finance] that all the blame [for the lost peace] fell once more on the Duc de Beauvilliers. Frankly [I believe] that the duke should rather have been praised for having dared to tell the king some very disagreeable truths; and that being in the service of the king impelled him [as a good counselor of the king] to speak. In the end the ministers . . . were all attacked [by His Majesty].

THE MINISTER RECEIVES A REPRIMAND BUT WINS A POINT [8]
27 January 1710

The king put off any decision [on peace terms] until Wednesday the 29th, at which time the council was to meet. I

[8] *Ibid.*, pp. 124–25.

reminded His Majesty that at that time a choice of ambassadors
[to be sent to the Netherlands] must be made. I asked him if
he still intended to employ the Abbé de Polignac. He replied
that he did, but added angrily, his face blotched red, that he did
not mean to send President Rouillé again because Rouillé was
so discredited [with the Allies] that the king's court would object to that choice. . . . [The king and his council] had searched
the year before for Rouillé's replacement but the king's ministers had made use of Rouillé [at that time] because they could
not find a suitable replacement; and, besides, that Monsieur
Chamillart [then Louis XIV's war minister] supported Rouillé
in the council. Meantime the ministers had searched unsuccess-
fully in the list of candidates for a successor. Nothing had happened for ten months. Now Rouillé must be excluded; even
Monseigneur [Louis XIV's son] had accepted the king's decision.
The council had then concluded that two plenipotentiaries must
be sent [to the Dutch], and that the first must be a prominent nobleman. The king, having at one time promised the post
to the Marshal d'Huxelles, was still inclined to appoint him.
All these matters, however, [Louis insisted] must be put off until
Wednesday.

Meanwhile, time was so precious that I gave in easily to the
advice given me by the Duc de Beauvilliers, namely to propose
to the king that his ministers consult on this important matter
[of the choice of ambassadors] the next day before the Finance
Council met. Beauvilliers pointed out that it would thus be
possible to send off a courier to The Hague [that day]. . . .

I broached the problem that same evening. But frankly the
Duc de Beauvilliers' suggestion was badly received by the king,
who thought it ridiculous that anyone could imagine that one
day more or less made any difference in a negotiation of this
sort. [As was often the case] he became irate with those who had
pressed him on matters of state. [In this instance] His Majesty
felt his counselors' excessive desire [for peace] had revealed to
the enemy that [France] would conclude a treaty at any price.
These reproaches fell principally on M. de Beauvilliers, who
His Majesty singled out, but I too was roundly scolded for having urged upon His Majesty that necessity of reaching a decision
[in the matter of ambassadors] before the Duke of Marlborough
and Prince Eugene arrived at The Hague. . . . The king added

[ironically] that he much admired my new-found zeal—I who was the slowest of all men in carrying out negotiations. I confess that I did not grasp the reason for His Majesty's reproach, nor why I deserved it, for I had never delayed the execution of his orders; in fact I anticipated them. But since masters believe themselves never to be in the wrong, I held my tongue and tried to profit from this mortification. . . .

The above encounter took place in Madame de Maintenon's rooms. From her bed she [called out] urging the king to think of finishing an affair so important as that of peace. [For a time] he resisted [our combined efforts], he debated the issues again, and finally surrendered, telling me to bring the necessary papers the next morning to the meeting of the Finance Council.

7

The King's Critics

Though Bishop Jacques Bénigne Bossuet (1627–1704) has been branded by some historians as a panderer to an absolute prince and as an apologist for a divine-right despot, the letter selected here, written shortly after his appointment as preceptor to Louis's son, shows Bossuet to be more than a political hack; indeed it singles him out as one of Louis XIV's first and most perceptive critics. Bossuet urges the king to remember that justice and mercy are essential attributes of kingship; that "the throne you fill belongs to God . . . and that you must rule according to his laws"; that God has imposed on the king the obligation of caring for his people's welfare and that Louis will be held accountable to the Deity for his stewardship. "May the gloire be to God" hardly sounds like the words of a sycophantic courtier.

THE BISHOP REMINDS THE KING OF HIS DUTY TO GOD[1]

You were born, Sire, with an intense love for justice, with a goodness and kindness which cannot be sufficiently esteemed; and it is in these things that God has included the greatest part of your duties, according to which we learn by this word of His Scripture: "Mercy and justice keep the king, and his throne is made firm by goodness and clemency." You must therefore consider, Sire, that the throne that you fill belongs to God, that you are keeping his place there, and that you must rule according to his laws. The laws that He has given you say that among your subjects, your power may be terrible only to those who are bad, and that your other subjects may live in peace and tranquillity while showing you obedience. Your peoples expect, Sire, to see you practice more than ever these laws that the Scriptures give

---

[1] From J. Standring, *Bossuet, A Prose Anthology* (London: George G. Harrap, 1962), pp. 207–17. Translated by J. Standring. Reprinted by permission of the publisher.

to you. The high profession that your Majesty has made of wishing to change in his life that which displeased God, has filled your people with consolation: it is persuading them that by your Majesty's giving himself to God, he will become more than ever attentive to the very strict obligation which He imposes on you to look after their misery, and it is from there that they are hoping for the relief for which they have an extreme need.

I am not unaware, Sire, how difficult it is to give them this relief in the midst of a great war in which you are obligated to such extraordinary expenses, both for resisting your enemies and for keeping your allies. But the war which obligates your Majesty to such great expenses obligates him at the same time not to let the people be weighted down by him alone who can support them. Thus their relief is as necessary for your service as for their peace. Your Majesty is not unaware of this; and to tell him in this question what I think his precise and indispensable obligation is, he must, above all else, apply himself to understanding the miseries of the provinces, and above all, what they must suffer without your Majesty's profit, as much through the disorders of the men of war as by the expense they go to to raise tax money, for which the farmers go to incredible excesses. Although your Majesty certainly knows, without doubt, how many injustices and extortions are committed in all these things, that which buoys up your peoples, Sire, is that they cannot persuade themselves that your Majesty knows everything and they hope that the application that he has shown for the things concerning his safety will oblige him to go deeply into such a necessary matter.

It is not possible for such great evils, which are capable of undermining the State, to be without remedy; otherwise, all would be lost without resource. But these remedies can only be found with much care and patience: because it is difficult to imagine practicable expedience, and it is not for me to discourse on these things. But what I know very certainly is that your Majesty bears witness with perseverance that he wants these things: if despite the difficulty which exists in detail, he persists invincibly in wanting what we are looking for: if finally he gives the impression, as he well knows how to do, that he does not want to be deceived on this subject and that he will be content with only solid and effective things: those to whom he gives the execution will bend to his will and will turn all their intelligence to satisfying him in the most just inclination that he may ever have.

Moreover, your Majesty, Sire, must be persuaded that however good the intentions of those who serve you for the relief of his peoples may be, it will never equal yours. Good kings are the true fathers of peoples; he loves them naturally: their glory and their most essential interests is in conserving them and doing them good, and the others will never be more forward in this than they. It is, therefore, your Majesty who, by the invincible force with which he wishes this relief, will bring to bear a similar desire in those that he employs: by never tiring of searching and of penetrating, he will finally see an effective result. The knowledge that he has of the affairs of his State and his exquisite judgment will make him disentangle that which is solid and real from that which is only apparent. Thus the evils of the State will be on the way to reparation, and the enemies who are hoping only for disorders caused by the impotence of your people will see themselves deprived of this hope. If that happens, Sire, will there ever be a prince more happy than you, or a reign more glorious than yours?

It has often happened that kings have been told their peoples are natural complainers, and that it is not possible to content them, whatever one might do. Without going very far back in the history of past centuries, our own has seen Henri IV, your grandfather, who by his clever and persevering goodness in looking for remedies for the evils of the State, had found the means of making the people happy, and of making them feel and confess their happiness. Thus he was loved for this with passion; and at the time of his death, one saw throughout the whole kingdom and in every family, I do not say astonishment, horror, and indignation, which such a sudden and execrable blow must have inspired, but a sadness similar to that which the loss of a good father causes his children. There is not one of us who does not remember having heard often-told this universal wailing from his father or his grandfather, and who does not still have his heart softened by what he has heard of the goodness of this king toward his people, and of extreme love of his people toward him. It is thus that he won over hearts; and if he had removed from his life the spot that your Majesty has just erased, his glory would be accomplished and he would be proposed as the model of a perfect king. It is not to flatter your Majesty by telling him that he was born with greater qualities than the former. Yes, Sire, you were born to draw from near and far the love and respect of all your peoples. You must assume this noble object of being feared only by the enemies of the State and by those who do evil. Let the rest love you, place in you their consolation and their hope and receive from your goodness, relief from their ills. It is that which of all your obligations is without doubt the most essential; and may your Majesty pardon me if I insist so much on this subject, which is the most important of all.

I know that peace is the real time to accomplish all these things; but as the necessity of waging and supporting a large war requires also the conservation of the people's energy, I do not doubt, Sire, that your Majesty may do it more than ever; and in the next winter quarter, as well as in all other things, one may see appear from your care and your compassion all the benefits which the conditions of the times may permit. It is that, Sire, which God orders you, and which he demands all the more from you since He has given you all the qualities necessary to carry out such a beautiful design: penetration, firmness, goodness, sweetness, authority, patience, vigilance, and assiduity in work. May the glory be to God who has given you all these gifts and who will demand their reckoning from you. You have all these qualities, and never was there a reign in which the people have more right to hope that they will be happy than in yours. Pray, Sire, to this great God, that he may give to you this grace, and that you may accomplish this great precept of St. Paul which requires kings to support their peoples as much as they can, mildly and peacefully, in all holiness and chastity.

We will work, however, to put Mgr le Dauphin in a position to succeed you and to profit from your examples. We often remind him of the very instructive letter that your Majesty wrote him. He reads and rereads it along with the one that followed, so powerful in impressing upon his mind the instructions of the first. It seems to me that he is trying in good faith to profit from this: and in fact, I notice something more serious in his conduct. I pray to God without cease that He give to your Majesty and to him His holy benedictions: and that He preserve your health in this strange time which gives us so much disquiet. God has at all times in His hand, and uses to advance and to slow down, as it pleases Him, the execution of men's designs. It is necessary to adore in everything His holy will, and to learn to serve Him for the love of Him.

I beg your Majesty to forgive me this long letter: never would I have had the boldness of speaking to him of these things if he had not expressly commanded it. I am telling him of things in general; and I leave to him their application, accordingly as God will inspire him. I am, with a respect and an absolute dependence, as well as with an ardor and an extreme zeal, etc., . . .

AN ARCHBISHOP CHASTISES THE KING [2]

> *Priest, mystic, courtier, François de Salignac de la Mothe-Fénelon (1651–1715) became one of Louis XIV's most implacable foes after having been one of his staunchest defenders. The transformation occurred in the years 1695–97 when Fénelon, the preceptor to the heir presumptive, the Duke of Burgundy, became embroiled in a controversy with Bishop Bossuet over matters of church dogma. In the Quietist controversy Fénelon espoused an unorthodox position, thus offending the king, who passionately disliked "all novelties" in religion. Fénelon was soon thereafter banished to his see at Cambrai. From his eerie in the archepiscopal palace Fénelon wrote letters severely critical of the king's policies, sending many of them secretly to his friend at court, the Duke of Chevreuse. In the letter printed here Fénelon complains bitterly of the king's failure to make a peace treaty with the Allies, led by an Anglo-Dutch coalition, who in the summer of 1710 were preparing to invade France. "Our great misfortune," Fénelon sighs, is "that one cannot lead the king through reasonable argument. . . . Our government policies are always behind times!"*

You will tell me that the king is incapable of resorting to such means [as the reformation of his government], that no one is close enough to him to propose these expedients and that he

[2] Fénelon, Letter to the Duc de Chevreuse, 4 August 1710. From Aimé-Martin, ed., *Oeuvres de Fénelon* (Paris: Firmin Didot Frères, Fils et Cie, 1861), Vol. III, pp. 647–49. Translated by J. C. Rule.

is not even in fit shape for consulting, questioning, or controlling the different men around him, or of comparing their diverse projects and deciding among their numerous opinions. To that I say it is indeed sad that strong medicine being the only method to save the sick man, [it is a pity] the sick man has neither the strength to take his medicine nor the strength to bear the results. If the king is too estranged [from good advice] to accept this expedient then he is a stranger as well to the welfare of the State; if he is incapable of employing the last measure of our resources in supporting the war without hope of obtaining peace, what more can we hope from him? If the approaching ruin of his throne does not open his eyes, does not make him move quickly against this danger, if he does not make haste to change his government, is not all lost? How can you say that the king sees the hand of God, and profits from humility [in the face of defeat], if an excess of arrogance makes him reject the single solution that remains for him now that he is at the edge of the abyss? The course of action that I propose would not be cowardly nor weak: on the contrary, it would be a courageous reaffirmation of order, justice, and true greatness. When will this happen if he obstinately refuses to come to a decision in this crisis, especially when at any moment we may all be doomed?

Now is the time that Monseigneur the Duke of Burgundy must speak to the King and to the dauphin[3] with all due respect but with firmness and with cautiously confidential manner, telling the king and dauphin all the things no one else had dared say to them. He must speak out in front of Madame de Maintenon; he must take the Duchess of Burgundy into his confidence; he must make it obvious that he speaks without being forced to do so by others; he must show that all will be lost if [financial] credit is not reestablished, but that credit can be reestablished only by a change of administration, which will convince the entire nation that it is up to them to support a monarchy faced with disaster whose king is willing to act for the nation's good. The Duke of Burgundy will probably be blamed, criticized, rejected out-of-hand: but his reasons for acting will be evident; his good sense will prevail little by little and it will save the throne of his fathers. He must risk displeasing the king and the dauphin to prevent them from destroying themselves. In the

[3] The Duke of Burgundy's father; Louis XIV's son.

final analysis what will he have done? He will have shown as
surely as two and two make four the truth and the necessity of
his advice; he will convince them with his zeal and his meek-
ness. Men will see that he speaks not from weakness nor timidity
but with a foresight and courage that will meet each test. At the
same time he can in all earnestness seek permission to join the
army as a volunteer. That is the true means to restore his reputation and to draw to himself the love and the respect of the
French people. Our great misfortune is that one cannot lead the
king through reasonable argument to accept a clear and quick
decision concerning the problems he must meet; one can never
make the king think except in slow degrees and by following
his customary patterns of thought, which, of course, causes decisions to come too late. Thus our governmental policies are
always behind times: we do today, and with great reluctance,
what we should have done two years ago; and we will be doing
in two years what we should have done today. For eighteen
months we have had to negotiate as slowly with the king, in
order to guide him to the goal [of making peace], as with the
enemy to reconcile them to sit down at the same peace table.
These two negotiations jostle each other, one or then the other
lagging behind: the king was not ready when the enemy was,
then the enemy was no longer willing to negotiate when the king
just began to be ready. But unfortunately the enemy has learned
to better adjust his claims to match his military means than the
king adjusts his views to the extremity to which, judging by
appearances, we are driven.

You will say that if a change of heart [in our king and govern-
ment] does not come a total collapse will follow. I answer that
God knows what I do not and that we will either find a new
courage or we will be overwhelmed without being destroyed.
God sees in the wealth of His providence the exact means that my
feeble reason cannot uncover. I love what He will do without
comprehending it; I await His decision. He knows with what
tenderness I love my country, with what gratitude and what
respectful affection I would give my life for that of the king,
with what zeal and feeling I am attached to the royal house and
especially to Monseigneur the Duke of Burgundy; but I cannot
hide my heart: it is due to this strong, tender, and constant feel-

ing that I wish that our terrible troubles will bring about the real cure of our political ills so that this violent crisis will not be without fruit.

You can best judge whether this letter be useful to you, my good Duke, and to My Lord the Duke of Beauvilliers. I might even dare hope that you will speak—with the utmost care, naturally—to Monseigneur the Duke of Burgundy, relating to him the contents of this letter that you believe will be useful and that will not upset him. It is not wise at this point to open his eyes to the king and the government. It will suffice to show the Duke of Burgundy what is necessary to give him strength to speak with cogency. God alone must give him, little by little, the remaining strength. Man must leave to God the finishing touches. . . .

HIS MOST CHRISTIAN MAJESTY LAMPOONED [4]

A vast outpouring of foreign pamphlet literature, some adulatory, but most of it hostile to Louis XIV, was triggered in the last decade of the seventeenth century and the early eighteenth century by the Revocation of the Edict of Nantes (1685) and by the French devastations in the Rhineland (1688–89). After a respite at the end of the War of the League of Augsburg and during the making of the Partition Treaties (1698–1700), the pamphlet war raged anew with the opening campaigns of the War of the Spanish Succession (1701 and after). The selections presented here are taken from a sketch of Louis's character and policies appended to a history of his life that appeared in London in 1709. The anonymous author quotes at length from the doggerel familiar to the populace of the period, contending that Louis's sins far outweigh his virtues: the king is condemned for his ambitions, for his vainglory, his "Romish Cruelty and Superstition," his lack of personal bravery, etc. The indictment of Louis's foreign policy is even more explicit: he is lampooned as the "Giver" of the peace at Nijmegen [Nimeguen], as the "Pacific Conqueror" whose aggressive actions led to the barbarous bombardment of Genoa,

[4] From *The Life and History of Lewis XIV present King of France and Navarre, Anon.* (London: John Morphew, 1709), "An Appendix containing the Character of the Most Christian King, His Virtues and Vices, . . ." pp. 5–8, 15–18, 23–24, 26, 29–30, 41.

the siege of Luxembourg, and the ravishing of the Palatinate
area of Germany. Truly his Most Christian Majesty!

Tho' it be no easy Matter to give a Just Character of the
Mind and Person of this Prince, I must say something of both.
He is tall and his Shoulders large, his Leg very fine, and
proportionable to his Body, which now is not very fat and never
was lean. He danc'd and perform'd all other Exercises in his
young days, beyond most, if not all the young Lords of his Court.
His Hair almost Black, mark'd a little with the Small Pox, his
Eye penetrating and insinuating and his Lips of a good Colour;
and for all that, his Face rather Majestick than Beautiful. A
great deal of Wit and excellent Natural Endowments; sparing
of his own Treasure and greedy of other People's. A Prudent
Manager of his Revenue, and yet not grudging the greatest
Sums, to accomplish his Designs; By which Means he has always
not only had Pensioners and Spies in all the Courts of Europe,
but many great Princes themselves have been his Pensioners.
Extravagantly Generous to his Mistresses and his Greatest
Favorites. A great Encourager of all Arts and Sciences. Firm in
his Resolutions where they can be executed without Prejudice to
his Interests. Love and Ambition his Predominant Inclinations.
But the latter Superior to all others: As being brought up in
the Opinion that Every thing is Lawful that is Beneficial; and
that Nothing can be Unlawful that is Convenient. Without faith
either to his own Subjects or other Nations, any further than
Interest and Necessity compel him to be so: Whence it may be
observ'd that the great Rewards he has sometimes conferr'd
upon his Generals and Ministers, have proceeded more out of a
principle of Policy than Gratitude: Which is confirm'd, not only
by the barbarous and treacherous Persecution of the Protestants,
but by the Neglect in which some great Men and their Posterity
have languish'd, when they cou'd be no more useful. His Valour
has been the Subject of many Panegyricks, Orations, Declama-
tions and what not: Yet I cannot find any Instance of personal
Bravery in all his Reign. Tho' he has always been sparing of
his own Flesh, he never had any regard to the Lives of his
Soldiers, whom he has strangely exposed to all the Inconvenien-
cies of Heat and Cold, etc. for the Advancement of his Designs;

And then by an affected Concern, a flattering Letter or some Insignificant piece of Generosity, he procures to himself the Admiration of the Army. He is severe in Discipline, and Inexorable in point of Infidelity or Cowardice; It is much less by his real Strength or the Bravery of his Troops, than by the Celerity of their Motions, the Severity of Discipline, the Secrecy of his Councils, and the Charms of his Money (which on those Occasions he never spared) that he has augmented his Dominions above one Third more than he received from his Predecessor. Perhaps if his Education had been less Narrow, and those about him fit for such a Task, he might really have been a Hero; wanting none of the Accomplishments that Nature can bestow.

The Cruelties of his Reign are Innumerable, and Black as Hell it self: But I have already said he was never taught Obedience to any other Law but that of his Interest and his Will. And if it be consider'd that being himself a Stranger to Learning and Religion, and Educated in the darkest Principles of the Romish Cruelty and Superstition, his Subserviency to the designs of what they call Holy Church will not be so much wondred at.

It ever has been easy for all his Subjects but the Protestants to have Access to the King; and when the Petitions are such as it consists with his Interest to give a favourable Answer to, he does it so obligingly, that the Manner heightens very much the Favour.

He has always affected an Uncommon Affability to Strangers, and been very Civil to such as visit his Court. His Deportment is indeed Majestick; But it is remarkable, that tho' he greatly affects a smiling and contented Look, it has often been observed by the Distraction of his Eyes, that every thing did not seem to be at ease within: For Kings it seems, and the greatest Kings must be Subject to the unerring Tribunal of their Consciences as well as other Men. Yet this great King wou'd never allow other Men to follow the Dictates of their own Consciences; But the Law of his Will.

The King's Vanity

His Vanity is proportionable to his Ambition, and that as Unbounded as the Desires of the Soul of Man can be. For he has not only suffer'd, but encourag'd the erecting of Statues, and making of Inscriptions and Devices upon them, which can hardly be outdone by the Pagan Antiquity; and which, however taking it may be with the ignorant Sort of that Airy Nation, yet must infinitely disgust all Impartial Men, and more expose the King's Weakness than enhance his Glory.

And so deeply has this Weakness of the King affected all that Nation, that ev'n the most Impartial of their Writers are Partial to the Advantage of their Prince: And particularly the famous Count de Bussy Rabutin, otherwise Inferior in all manner of Accomplishments to few Men in France, has in what he has written of the King, derogated so far from the Veracity and Generosity so visible in the rest of his Writings, that it hardly seems to be the same Author.

No French Prince has ever been more Magnificent than he, and indeed since Charlemagne none has had the Means to be so: Of which the famous Carrousel in 1662, the Palaces of Versailles, Marly, the Louvre, and several others built or imbellish'd by him, are sufficient Evidences; Not to mention the Camp at Compiegne; . . .

Nor was that Scepter ever wielded by a Prince, who better understood the Art of Commanding nor had an Education more unfit to qualify him for it. To which I must add, that however much he has oppressed his Subjects himself, he has excell'd all those that have gone before him in reforming all Abuses either in the Law it self, or in the Practice of it: And that he has Enacted better new Laws and provided better for the Execution of them than all his Predecessors. Witness the Edicts for the Abolishing of Duels, the Ordinances about Bankruptcy and about Fishing, Exchange, Navigation and Trade in all it's Branches; which no Nation under the Sun can Parallel.

Now if from the Story of that Monarch's Amours, we come to dissect the other Parts of his Character, we shall not find him so great a Man as the World has believ'd him to be.

I have already insinuated that his Personal Valour is much suspected; But he has left no room to doubt of the height of his Ambition, of which his whole History is one continued Proof. But instead of the real Valour and Grandeur of Soul, so Natural to Ambitious Men, the Efforts he has us'd to be thought the Man he really is not, has expos'd his Weakness and his Vanity to all Europe: Which Contagion from the Throne has so affected the People, that it now seems to be an Essential Part of their Character: Which has most authentickly appear'd in the many nauseous, both publick and private Flatteries and Absurdities they have been guilty of, and which their natural Lightness prompts them to, to increase and magnify (as they fancy) THE GLORY of their Prince, which they hardly seem to think Inferior to that of God Almighty. Nor have they ever spar'd to do that ev'n at the Expence of their best Allies, whose Mistakes it was certainly their Interest to conceal: It is not to be denied but King Charles II. of England was much overseen[5] in Selling Dunkirk; which is a Port that cou'd hardly be sold for its worth. However one wou'd have thought that the Gentlemen of the French Academy of Inscriptions shou'd have been a little more Politick than to expose the Weakness of King Charles to his Parliament and to all Europe, in a blustering Medal in which they tell us, that for Five Millions (about 400,000 Pound) his Majesty had purchas'd of the English the Town of Dunkirk, one of the most considerable in the Low Countries. From which time they Date their Security, and the Flourishing Condition of the Kingdom.

But besides that and many other Publick Medals, struck by Authority, and more largely taken Notice of in the Body of this Discourse, many others have been made by Private Persons; either to flatter the Court or please Themselves.

In one of these representing the second Conquest, or rather the second Stealing of the City of Besçançon,[6] they tell us, That what Caesar cou'd do but Once, the Great Lewis has done Twice: Adding, that Nothing is impossible to the Valour of the French; that Victory is in their Pay, and serves them in Quality of Thunder-Carrier. But it seems of late Years, they have detain'd her Arrears, or else she has very foully Jaded them.

THE SUN'S RADIANCE DIMS [7]

Nothing is more Natural to the French than to compare their Prince, to his Darling Device, THE SUN. They tell us, the one

[5] In 1662 Charles II sold Dunkirk to France.

[6] Besançon was the capital of the Free County of Burgundy (the Franche-Comté); both city and county were twice seized by Louis XIV, first in 1667–68, second in 1674. The treaty of Nijmegen awarded both city and county to France.

[7] *Ibid.*

goes with the same Rapidity as the other, from Conquest to Conquest, and from Glory to Glory: And tho' it be known to all Christendom that he has ever been its common Disturber; some Sycophant, upon the Conclusion of the Peace of Nÿmegen,[8] which Lewis XIV, was glad to Buy, represents him in a Medal, according to the Common, Impudent Phrase of the French, as the GIVER of that Peace, which when he had by his Money and his Fallacies obtain'd, he immediately after broke: And yet his Scandalous Flatterer calls him, The PACIFIER of the WORLD. Upon the barbarous and unprecedented Bombardments of the free City of Genoa,[9] and Attacking against the Faith of all Treaties, and against all the Laws of War and Honour, the Important City of Luxemburg,[10] in the time of a profound Peace; They place in a Medal their faithless Monarch, between Genoa and Luxemburg, with the Globe of the World upon the Point of his Sword, with this Motto, *Quad libet licet*: I can do with it what I Please. And on the other side, A Sword and a Branch of Olive, with this Motto, *Elige*: Chuse which you Please; Viz. Peace or War.

Upon the Birth of the Dauphin's second Son, the Duke of Anjou;[11] they struck a Medal with this Motto, The Eternity of the French Empire: Which they presum'd to say, was in a manner secur'd, by the Birth of a Second Heir.

In many other Medals, they have render'd the Terms of Perpetual Conqueror, Pacifier of the Universe, Father of the Country, &c. perfectly familiar to their Prince: And tho' all the World knows that France has Essential Obligations to the Swedes, who are under none to France; they represent Sweden, sheltering her self under the Wings of their Gallick Cock, with this Motto; Gallus Protector.

They vainly Ascribe to him in other Medals the Dominion of the Sea; ev'n after the Ruine of his Ships at La Hogue[12]: They Deaffen the World with the Stories of his Victories; and yet are so rediculous as to banter him over and over again, with the Name of Pacifick Conqueror: And in a Medal giv'n as the Price of Eloquence, to the Person that shou'd compose the finest Son-

[8] In 1678–79.
[9] In May 1684.
[10] In 1683.
[11] In August 1682.
[12] In 1692.

net, in Praise of the King, they represent him under the Figure of the Sun, dissipating the Clouds, and chasing away Night Birds and Monsters; with these Passages of the Psalms; which they do horridly Profane, for the Idol Glory of their Impious Monarch.

Louis the Great Taunted

Upon the Occasion of the Peace of Nimeguen, besides many other Vain Medals and Inscriptions; the two following are very observable.

> To Lewis the Great, who after Defeating the Hollanders, and Overcoming more than once the Spaniards; twice Conquering Franche Comté; Beating several times the Germans; and Chasing and Burning the Fleets of the Enemy, gave Peace to Europe, almost entirely conjur'd and confederated against him; and forc'd them to accept it upon his own Terms.

> Lewis the Great, by a rare Example of Moderation; Stopping the Course of his Victories, which open'd a large Field of new Conquests, and seem'd to assure him that Fortune was his Pensioner; after so many Successes, made it appear that he had only conquer'd to give Peace to the Christian World; since his Majesty was pleas'd to Sacrifice to that, the Advantages of his Victories.

This Place of Victory (as they call it) is Oval and almost of the Shape of the Place where the Dial is erected in the Center of Seven Streets in the Parish of St. Giles's Suburbs of London: But much better Pav'd, and the Houses infinitely more glorious, Built of fine Free Stone: Where, on the Fourteenth of March 1686, the aforesaid Duke,[13] who besides his other Places, was Buffoon and Flatterer in Ordinary to the King of France, erected a Glorious Statue to the utter Ruine of his Estate, which had not been sufficient to give his Son, the present Duke, Bread; if the King had not made him Amends by procuring him a good Marriage.

The King's Statue is, I think, 16 foot high, and stands upon a glorious square Pedestal of white Marble, which is full of Inscriptions; and at the four Corners of which are four Statues of Slaves in Chains, with the Arms of four Nations; whereof Complaint being made by some Ambassadors at Reswick,[14] the Great

[13] La Feuillade.
[14] Ryswick Peace Congress.

Lewis was forc'd to disown his Victorious Statue, which they said was set up without his Privity, and which he had never seen.

One of these Slaves represents the Turkish Pirates, and by the Three others, they presume to denote, so many European Powers, whom they falsely pretend to have Conquer'd: All the Figures being of Brass, and the Steps to the Pedestal environ'd with handsom Rails of Iron.

> To LEWIS the GREAT, The FATHER and LEADER of his ARMIES; Always VICTORIOUS
> For having subdu'd his Enemies, Protected his Allies, and added most Powerful Nations to his Dominions; Secured the Frontiers by Impregnable Forts, Joyn'd the Ocean and the Mediterranean, Scowr'd all the Seas of Pirates, Reform'd the Laws, extirpated Heresy; and by the Fame of his Actions, acquir'd the Admiration of the remotest Nations; Managing every thing to Perfection, at Home and Abroad, by the Greatness of his Genius and his Courage:

There are many other Vain-glorious Inscriptions, and there have not been wanting some who have wittingly Burlesqu'd them. Some of the most remarkable of which I have here collected. The following Distick was writ upon the Palace of Versailes [sic].

> Regia, Rex, Regnum, Tria funt miracula Mundi,
> Rex animo, Regnum viribus, Arte Domus.

> Satyrically Paraphras'd,

> King, Kingdom, Palace, are Three Wonders found,
> He's Mad, They Naked, This on Rotten Ground.

Upon the Gate of one of the Jesuit's Colleges in Paris they have struck out the Name of Jesus, which by the Rule of their Order, is to be set upon all their Buildings, and have put the King's Name in its stead; Upon which, one very wittingly writ thus,

> Abstulit hinc Jesum posuitque Insignia Regis,
> Impia Gens, Alium non habet illa Deum.

> Render'd,

> They Jesus Name have t'ane from their Abode,
> And plac'd the King's, He only is their God.

The two following Verses were made in Honour of the Great Lewis.

> Una Dies Lotheros, Burgundos Hebdomas una,
> Una Domat Battavos Luna; Quid annus Aget?

In one Day he conquer'd Lorain; Franche Comté (or the County of Burgundy) in a Week; the Dutch in a Month: What can't he do in a Year?

Burlesqu'd as 'tis said by the late E. of Rochester.

> Lorain he Stole, by Fraud he got Burgundy,
> Holland he bought and I'gad he sh'll pay for't one day.

In another Cut they represent Lewis XIV, in a Mortal Fright on an Eclipse of the Sun the 12th of May 1706 and Philip V's being driven out of Catalonia. That young Prince is drawn upon his Knees, Petitioning his Grandfather for Leave to come home again. And Madam de Maintenon advised Lewis le Grand to send the Confederates a Blank to procure a Peace.

> *Lou.* What shall we do, dear Maintenon? My Grand-Son
> Flies from the Foe, and we are all undon.
> Brabant and Flanders to the Austrian yield,
> So much we suffer'd when we lost the Field;
> O why am I thus wretched! *Maint.* To be plain,
> I'll tell you why, to Flatter you's in vain:
> The fam'd Partition-Treaty was the Cause,
> And England's just Resentment, and Nassau's:
> You own'd a Prince whom they refus'd to own,
> And poor Bavaria's by your Arts undone;
> You trickt the Portuguese. *Lou.* The Sun, my Dear
> Is now eclips'd and bodes some Ill, I fear.
> *Phil.* Good Grandsire, take me in again, my Fall
> Is great, and you have been the Cause of all.
> *Lou.* My Love, my Queen, now me what to do?
> For on thy Counsel I depend. *Maint.* Be true,
> Keep to your Word, forget your usual Fraud,
> For which you're curst at home and loath'd abroad,
> Send the Confederates a Blank. *Lou.* 'Tis done;
> What other way was left to save my Crown?

8
The Death of Louis XIV

By August 27, 1715, Louis XIV became con-
vinced that he would not recover from a gangrenous infec-
tion in his leg. He began at once to settle his mundane af-
fairs and to make peace with God. He called for his private
papers and burned many of them. (He had already destroyed
some personal correspondence in 1712 and again in 1714.)
Then he prepared for death. Saint-Simon assures us that the
king remained rational until the very end, even upbraiding
his servants saying: "Why are you crying? Did you think I
was immortal?" or exclaiming "As for restitutions I owe
nothing to any individual." Two of Louis's most famous
deathbed observations omitted by the usually omniscient
Saint-Simon are worth recording. When Louis's great-grand-
son (Louis XV) was led to the king's bedside, Louis urged
him to remember his duty to God and to avoid war, which
"I loved too much." A little later Louis was said to have
observed that though he was dying, the State would live on.
With these words Louis announced the emergence of the im-
personal, bureaucratic State of the modern era.

THE KING FACES DEATH WITH COMPOSURE [1]

On Tuesday, 27 August, no one entered the King's room,
save for Père Tellier, Mme de Maintenon, and, for his mass
only, Cardinal de Rohan, and the two almoners on duty. At
two o'clock, exactly, he sent for the Chancellor and, alone with
him and Mme Maintenon, made him open two boxes full of
papers, making him burn many of them, and giving him orders
for the disposal of the rest. At six o'clock in the evening, he asked
again for the Chancellor. Mme de Maintenon did not leave his
room the whole of that day, and no one else entered it except

[1] From *Historical Memoirs of the Duc de Saint-Simon* (London: Hamish
Hamilton, 1968), Vol. II, pp. 496–97, 497–98; ed. and trans. by Lucy Norton.
Reprinted by permission of the publisher.

the valets and, from time to time, those who were essential for his service. During the evening, he sent for Père Tellier and, almost immediately after, for Pontchartrain, commanding him to have his heart taken to the professed house of the Jesuits in Paris, as soon as he was dead, and to have it placed opposite to the heart of the King his father, and after the same manner. Shortly after that, he recollected that Cavoye, the grand-marshal of his household, had never yet had occasion to arrange for the Court to be in residence at Vincennes, for it was fifty years since they had last been there. He directed them to a box that contained a plan of that château, and commanded them to take it to Cavoye. Later on, when he had given these orders, he said to Mme de Maintenon that he had heard tell of the difficulty of resigning oneself to death; but that as he approached the awful moment, he did not find it too hard to submit. She replied that it must be very painful if one were attached to people, or hated them in one's heart, or had restitutions to make. "Oh!" said the King, "as for restitutions I owe nothing to any individual; and for what I owe to the kingdom, I trust in the mercy of God." The following night was terribly agitated. He could be seen continually pressing his hands together, and they heard him reciting the prayers which he had been wont to say when well, and beating his breast at the *Confiteor*.

On the morning of 28 August, he gave a word of comfort to Mme de Maintenon, which she so little relished that she did not answer. He said that the thought which consoled him in parting from her was the hope that, considering her age, they would soon be reunited. At seven that morning he had sent for Père Tellier and, as they spoke of God, he had seen reflected in the mirror above the chimney-piece two of his pages in tears, sitting at the foot of his bed. He said to them, "Why are you crying? Did you think I was immortal? I, myself, have never thought so, and considering my age, you should have been prepared to lose me."

For a short time he felt stronger; but when, his pulse being weak and almost failing, they offered him a second dose at four o'clock, saying that it would revive him, he answered as he took the glass, "Life or death, as God pleases." Mme de Maintenon had just left the room with her hood drawn down; the Maréchal de Villeroy led her past the door of her apartments, which she did not enter, and down the grand staircase, where she stopped and raised her hood. Then, completely dry-eyed, she embraced the Maréchal, saying, "Adieu, M. le Maréchal," and stepping into the King's coach that was always at her disposal and in which Mme de Caylus was waiting, she drove away to Saint-Cyr, followed by a second coach containing her women. That evening the Duc du Maine made an excellent story of Fagon's encounter with Le Brun. I shall return later to his conduct, and that of Mme de Maintenon and Père Tellier during the last days of the King's life. Le Brun's remedy continued to be given as he advised, and he was always present when the King took it. When they wished the King to drink some soup, he said that they should not speak to him as to other men; that what he needed was not soup but his confessor, and he had him recalled. One day when he came to his senses after a period of unconsciousness, he asked Père Tellier for general absolution from his sins, and Père Tellier inquired whether he suffered very much. "No, alas!" replied the King, "that is what distresses me; I should prefer to suffer more for the expiation of my sins."

The late evening did not fulfil the much vaunted promise of that morning, at which time the Curé of Versailles had taken advantage of the emptier room to tell the King that the people were praying for his life. The King had replied that it was not now a question of that, but of his salvation, for which prayers were badly needed. When he had given his orders that morning, he had let slip the words, "the young King," when speaking of the Dauphin. He observed the sudden movement among the onlookers and said, "Well, what of it? That does not trouble me at all." At eight o'clock he took some more of the elixir of that man from Provence. His head appeared to be confused, and he said himself that he felt very bad. At eleven, they examined his leg. Gangrene had spread all over his foot and knee, and his thigh was much swollen. He fainted during the examination. He was distressed to notice the absence of Mme de Maintenon, who had not intended to return. He asked for her several times during the day; and they were unable to conceal from him that she had gone. He sent to fetch her from Saint-Cyr; she returned in the evening.

Friday, 30 August was as distressing as the night before had been; a deep coma set in, and in the intervals his mind wandered.

From time to time he swallowed a little jelly in plain water, for he could no longer take wine. Only the valets essential for his service remained in the room with the doctors and Mme de Maintenon; Père Tellier appeared on rare occasions when Blouin or Maréchal summoned him. Few remained even in the studies; M. du Maine not amongst them. The King quickly responded to words of piety, when Mme de Maintenon or Père Tellier found the moments when his head was less confused; but such moments were rare and of short duration. At five that evening, Mme de Maintenon went to her apartments, distributed such furniture as belonged to her among the members of her staff, and departed to Saint-Cyr, never to return.

The day and the night of Saturday, 31 August, were horrible indeed. There were only brief and rare moments of consciousness. The gangrene had reached his knee and spread over this entire thigh. They gave him the late Abbé Aignan's remedy, which the Duchesse du Maine suggested as being an excellent thing against smallpox. By this time, the doctors were agreeing to anything because they had lost all hope. Towards eleven in the evening, they thought him so ill that the prayers for the dying were said over him. The bustle brought him to his senses. He recited the prayers in a voice so strong that it could be heard above those of the many priests, and above those of all the people who had entered with them. When the prayers ended he recognized Cardinal de Rohan and said to him: "Those are the last blessings of the Church." That was the last person to whom he spoke. He several times repeated, *"Nunc et in hora mortis,"* then said, "O God help me! Haste thou to succour me." Those were his last words. He lay unconscious throughout the night. His long agony ended at a quarter past eight, on the morning of Sunday, 1 September, 1715, three days before his seventy-seventh birthday, in the seventy-second year of his reign.

He had married at the age of twenty-two, after signing the famous Peace of the Pyrenees, in 1660. He was twenty-three when death delivered France of Cardinal Mazarin; twenty-seven, when he lost the Queen his mother, in 1666. He became a widower at forty-four, in 1683; lost Monsieur his brother when he was sixty-three, in 1701, and survived all his sons, grandsons and great-grandsons, excepting only his successor, the King of Spain, and the sons of that monarch. Europe had never known so long a reign, nor France so old a king.

PART THREE

LOUIS XIV IN HISTORY

Eighteenth-century historians usually espoused one of three interpretations or theses of Louis XIV's reign. The first was the noble thesis, *whose advocates criticized Louis XIV for having excluded the nobles from the king's councils, suggesting that such conduct was tantamount to tyranny. The second was the* royal thesis, *whose supporters urged reform "from above," and who saw Louis XIV as a forerunner of enlightened despotism; the third was the* democratic thesis, *whose adherents condemned Louis as an unreconstructed reactionary.*

A distinguished eighteenth-century advocate of the noble thesis *was the great political theorist and social critic, Baron de Montesquieu (1689–1755), who urged that the principal judges of France, the nobility of the robe, should assume the leadership of the nobility and form an intermediate body of power between the people and the king. Like Fénelon and Saint-Simon (Chapters 4, 7), Montesquieu accused Louis XIV of assuming the trappings of despotism; on this latter point his fellow philosophe Voltaire (1694–1778) disagreed and posited the* royal thesis *in his monumental work,* The Age of Louis XIV (1751). *As described by Voltaire Louis XIV appears an energetic ruler who, through such agents as Colbert, was dedicated to improving the lot of the average Frenchman. Voltaire's contemporary Jean-Jacques Rousseau (1712–78) quarreled with both Montesquieu's and Voltaire's views of Louis XIV. Rousseau, an advocate of the* democratic thesis, *believed that in time sovereignty would be held collectively by the people. To Rousseau, Louis XIV was a monster; Rousseau's progeny, the Jacobin republicans of the French Revolution, likewise despised the Grand Monarch; and even during the years of the Bourbon Restoration and the Orleans Monarchy (1815–48), the Sun King's reputation suffered because the conservatives of the early nineteenth century preferred to praise Louis's grandfather "good King Henri," or Louis XVI, the martyr of 21 January 1793, while largely neglecting "the sultan of Versailles."*

9
Classic Republican Accounts of the Nineteenth and Twentieth Centuries

Only in the last decades of the ninteenth century did Louis XIV achieve historiographical respectability, and this through the efforts of Ernest Lavisse (1842–1922) and his associates. A child of several political traditions, Lavisse, born during the reign of the Orleans dynasty, became tutor to the Prince Imperial (1869) and remained for some time after the fall of the Second Empire (1870) a confirmed Bonapartist. Later, under the Third Republic, Lavisse embraced republican ideas and became one of the chief educationalists of France, both as a professor at the Sorbonne and as director of the chief training center for civil servants, the École Normale Superieure. Writing in a semi-official "History of France," Lavisse set down for several generations the lines of interpretation of the "great century." Cautiously hostile to Louis XIV, Lavisse adapted the testimony of the Duke of Saint-Simon to the twentieth century. The Sorbonne professor agreed with Saint-Simon that Louis had been poorly educated in a formal sense and that his character as a ruler was molded chiefly by his view of the Frondes. Once Louis's personal rule had begun (1661) he was determined to quash incipient revolts before they began. In so doing Louis set himself above his ministers and advisers and was not embarrassed even by "God's presence." Louis's priests warned him that he was a mere mortal, but he obviously did not believe them. Both Lavisse and Saint-Simon agree that Louis was a master of the political gesture, who ruled France by spectacle, but that his divine-right absolutism was tempered by disobedience.

Like Lavisse, Philippe Sagnac (1868–1954) was a good re-

*publican, an admirer of middle-class virtues. But Sagnac
carries Lavisse's interpretation a step further: along with
Montesquieu, he believes that Louis came close to being a
tyrant in the oriental sense, a prince who wished to reduce
his people to absolute obedience, if not slavery. Clearly,
Louis also wanted to dominate Europe, not so much by
conquest as by fear. Grudgingly, however, Sagnac condones
Louis's policy toward the Germanies. Having been schooled
during the Franco-Prussian War, and having taught at the
Sorbonne during two twentieth-century German invasions
of France, Sagnac approves of Louis's attempts to close the
gates to Germany:* Clausa Germanis Gallia.

ERNEST LAVISSE: MÉTIER DE ROI [1]

Louis XIV's stately exterior masked prudence, circumspection and restraint. In his *Mémoires* he confesses a timidity caused
by a fear of saying or doing the wrong thing. During the time of
Cardinal Mazarin's ministry Louis worked hard to shape his own
opinions about the issues he heard discussed; and was proud
when he "could resolve them in a statesmanlike manner." Yet
even when he ruled he was often troubled by feelings of uncertainty. "Too often there are painful situations and delicate
circumstances to work out. . . ." He did not speak impromptu.
He memorized important speeches and hesitated if he forgot the
words. As he was discussing the Fouquet affair with members
of the Parlement an amusing thing happened. D'Ormeson, who
was there, related that "the king stopped speaking in order to
think about what he wanted to say. When the words failed to
come to him he told us 'It is vexing to have this happen, for in
matters such as this it is best to say only what one has been
planned to say.' Thus he impressed upon us the importance of
careful planning for 'in doubtful matters the only confident way
to act is to expect the worst.' He further expanded the maxim
that 'to cherish one's hopes is a bad principle.' "

Louis displayed a great royal virtue, that is, a joy in being king.

[1] From Ernest Lavisse, ed., *Histoire de France* (Paris: Libraire Hachette,
1911), Vol. VII, Part 2, pp. 4–9, trans. J. C. Rule. Reprinted by permission of
the publisher.

He let that joy be seen in his every act. "The kingship," he said, "is a grand, noble, and delightful profession."

This exuberant definition depended upon the king himself. Louis's chief honor was his understanding that this *"grandeur,"* "nobility," and "delight" depended upon work.

Colbert tells that in one day the young king presided over the Council of Finances from ten o'clock in the morning until one-thirty in the afternoon; dined, presided over another council; devoted two hours to learning Latin (he understood it poorly and wished to read the acts of the Pope's chancellery); and in the evening held a third council until ten o'clock. That day was not untypical.

When working he did not close himself up in his study or sit meditatively with his head between his hands. His work consisted above all of the attention he gave to councils, ministers, numerous audiences, and men whose opinions he valued. . . . He gave the same attention to less important political affairs, and took the same care in listening to the Marshal de Bellefonds talk about "the particular inclinations of the women at court" as he took in discussing grand designs of war with the Marshal de Turenne. He watched all that happened around him while retaining an aura of composure. Everything revolved around the king. The court was in a constant state of turmoil and the ministers always made their concerns known to him. Whoever may have seen Colbert and Lionne moving through the corridors for the first time would probably have said the same thing the La Bruyère wrote later concerning Colbert and Lionne: "No one ever saw them sitting still, but whoever has seen them working? The young master goes from one thing to another with such ease that one can hardly believe this is the same prince."

Yet Louis quickly tired of dividing his attention among so many different roles. He was vigorous, enduring great physical exertion. He showed little strain, even on bad days; but since childhood he suffered from stomach and intestinal disorders. In 1662, he had an attack of dizziness, general queasiness, weakness, despondency and general melancholy. No doubt his gluttonous appetite, his customary guzzling of food and bad teeth suffice to explain the physical disorder but the ambassador from Venice who witnessed "the loss of color in the king's face" wrote in

1665, that "he gets emotionally caught up in his work and is apprehensive about those who might destroy his good name. He becomes mentally fatigued and thus succumbs to violent headaches."

However, neither sickness, nor the medicine (more to be feared than the sickness itself) interfered with the regime of his daily life. For a half century he followed the same routine. Saint-Simon later wrote, "with the aid of an almanac and a watch one could predict what the king was doing at any given moment, even if he be three hundred leagues away." This unchanging orderliness in his working habits seemed to be a natural law. . . .

And he loved explanations. Colbert, who has been accused of drowning the king in details, always explained things to the king several times. He understood that the way to win the king's favor was to report everything to the smallest detail. But Louis seldom had the insight to search out problems. Because of his deplorable education he seldom could see beyond the obvious.

Education

Louis XIV had been a poor student because his principal teacher Cardinal [Mazarin] was the least qualified man to instruct him. The circumstances of his youth—civil war, riots, escapes, cavalcades and battles—were further impediments. He learned very little from his instructors. "It is disheartening not to know what is common knowledge," the king said in regard to his ignorance of history. There is no doubt, however, that he did receive a professional education.

Louis saw war at firsthand and withstood the ordeal well. Each year he appeared with the armies, joyfully withstanding the inconveniences and deprivations, riding for fifteen hours at a time and taking part in various skirmishes. During the siege of Dunkirk in May, 1658, he wished to stay despite the pleadings of the queen and the cardinal who feared the visit to a place infested by dead bodies half interred in the sand from earlier battles; he appeared at the exposed positions giving orders to advance the siege work. The following month at the siege of Berques-Saint-Winox he fell ill. He hid his illness from the cardinal as long as possible. Upon finally hearing of it the cardinal took great pains to get permission to have him sent to Calais. There the worst happened: during the night of July 6–7 he received communion and bravely said to the cardinal, "You are a man of resolution and the best friend that I have. Therefore I beg you to warn me when I am in extremis." Testimony of the time leaves little doubt as to the young king's qualities of endurance and courage and his overwhelming desire to learn the art of war. He attended the councils of war and took lessons from Turenne and from the cardinal who was considered a man of genius in military affairs. During the peace that followed [1659] Louis delighted in exercising his troops: putting them through maneuvers, and reviewing them corps by corps, company by company, and man by man. . . .

Louis also grasped [with ease] foreign affairs. Colbert wrote that one day, during the earlier years of his personal reign, Louis held an audience with the Spanish ambassador. The ambassador wished to discuss the problem of negotiating with the French ministers but the king began to review his own complaints about the court of Spain. The ambassador tried, at every pause in the king's discourse, to get a word in, but the king would only rephrase his complaints. The Spanish ambassador was astonished and said that in working with kings for 40 years he had never before known one who spoke in anything other than monosyllables.

Under Mazarin's tutelage Louis became acquainted with the stratagems of French politics. . . . Mazarin taught him the necessity of sacrificing every scruple, even honor, for the sake of reason of state. From Louis the cardinal wrested consent for an alliance with Cromwell, that regicide, a stratagem that was repugnant to the king. Mazarin showed Louis skill of governing, the art of bribing ministers and even princes, the price of a vote of an elector in the Holy Roman Empire or that of a cardinal in the Roman Catholic Church. And finally Mazarin showed him how the election of the two heads of the Christian world, the Pope and the Emperor, was largely a matter of intrigue. Under such tutelage the king, unfortunately for the future, acquired a scorn for foreign governments.

Foreign and military affairs were indeed important parts of the government but there were other matters about which, because of his own ignorance, Mazarin was unable to teach Louis. The cardinal asked only that he might be furnished with enough money to accomplish his policies and whims. His philosophy of governing was severely limited; in the last advice to the king [on his death bed] he recommended that he "comfort his people as much as resources would allow, support the church in its rights, immunities, and privileges as one would an oldest son, and consider the nobility his right arm." He might just as well have said nothing at all.

Mazarin handled the domestic side of government as he did diplomacy. His first principle was to distrust everyone. He told the king when he was a child that "His majesty must realize that he cannot trust a Frenchman" because every Frenchman was interested only in weakening the king's power. . . .

Louis knew the price of his subjects' fidelity. "There was scarcely any of my subjects whose loyalty cannot be purchased by money or promises of honor." And thus the king was forced to pretend to lie, even at times to become a comedian.

The idea of a king as universal benefactor and patron is expressed in [Louis XIV's] *Mémoires*:

"All eyes are directed toward the King, and he alone is the object of all petitions; he alone receives respect; he alone is the object of all hopes; everything that is done is subject to his approval; his esteem is looked upon as the font of favor. One measures one's importance by one's closeness to the king and by the esteem in which he holds you. Everything else is without meaning."

A king who by means of anticipated favors holds the great world of his courtiers in obedience and submission to his will no longer need worry as to how he governs. Louis XIV, in fact, believed it easy and even amusing to rule and therein is where he made some of his gravest errors.

These errors, indeed, he was wont to transmit to his son: "You should not think that affairs of state are similar to the obscure and thorny sciences which have exhausted [the patience] of many. . . . The function of kingship consists mainly in allowing good sense to act naturally and without fear of restraint. What occupies our time is often not as difficult as we would at first imagine. . . . What is most necessary to our job is at the same time [often] pleasant. In a word, my son, one must keep one's eyes open, listen with great care to the news from each province and nation, to the secrets from every court, to [learn of] the temper and the weakness of every prince and foreign minister; it is a matter of being aware of an infinite number of things that many people believe we unaware of, of discovering what is hidden from us with such care, of discovering the most obscure point of view of our courtiers; I know of no greater pleasure than learning what curiosity leads one to discover."

Government by Spectacle

Government, then, is a spectacle; and the spectacle was one of the great pleasures of the seventeenth century. The men of that time loved to see the passions and the absurdities of the day played out on the stage by actors, and further acted by themselves wherever they might meet, at court or in the city. The men of the seventeenth century were observers, and, as we would say today [amateur] psychologists. . . . The greatest spectacle was provided by the king himself, who took great pleasure in it; he gathered around him all the world: provinces, nations, courts, and princes. Louis XIV never grew weary of watching and listening. No one has ever evinced greater insatiability for news, be it important or not. Yet, it is certainly true that a king must watch with care and be well informed. . . . Yet Louis XIV did not discover [in time] that affairs of states, like the sciences, do have their obscure and thorny side; thus, in the declining years of his reign, he often wept during the evening he spent with Mme. de Maintenon the heavy tears of winter which dried less quickly than those of spring.

[Yet withal] Louis XIV—and this is apparent from his very first words and gestures—found in his own person the principle [of governing] and the end-in-itself. . . . He believed in himself as a very act of faith. If he did indeed utter the words "L'État c'est moi," what he meant to say quite simply was "I, Louis, speak to you."

Louis XIV was never [properly] instructed in religious dogma. . . . His mother and his confessors taught him a pious attitude toward life: he said his prayers morning and evening, he attended mass every day; he listened with concentration to long and numerous sermons and required the young courtiers to be present at chapel and to give at least outward signs of devotion. His reasons, however, for loving religion remained, throughout his life, highly personal. . . . His birth had been hailed as a miracle: after long years of sterility King Louis XIII and Queen Anne had, after many devotions and prayers, accomplished their desire: an heir. Louis XIV was thus given the name "the Godgiven." In recognition of this miracle Queen Anne dedicated the church of Val-de-Grâce to "the baby Jesus and the Virgin Mother." Louis was constantly told [as he grew up] that he was the Most Christian King and the Eldest Son of the Church. Louis believed these things implicitly, and sincerely thought himself blessed among men, one who stood near to God.

God's presence did not embarrass Louis XIV. The priests told him that he was but a mere mortal and would return to dust, but he did not believe them. Did they themselves believe it? Louis heard them say that he was God's image on Earth. "O kings! You are like Gods!" He defined his duties toward the Deity by such single-minded maxims. "God is infinitely jealous of his Glory. He endowed us with superior talents so that we can honor him the more." Thus Louis XIV, with evident sincerity, and without embarrassment, established between God and himself a mutual understanding and need. He believed God, in certain ways, had need of him and after he recorded his first successes the king added that he felt himself obliged to thank God. He [subsequently] enumerated all his acts of gratitude toward God: the rules adopted to "reduce the people of the Pretended Reformed Religion" [that is, the Protestants], to the exact terms of the Edict of Nantes; the prohibition on Protestant religious assemblies; the alms given to the poor of Dunkirk in order to bring them back into the Catholic fold; the agreements with the Dutch in favor of the Catholics in the Guelderland, and the dispersion of the "religious communities where the Jansenists' ideas are fomented." Altogether Louis had a rather poor image of God as a Deity who was consumed by a passion for Glory, just like any miserable mortal, and, on the other hand, Louis had a very high estimate of himself. . . . For instance the king wanted us to know that on the occasion of a Jubilee "he followed a religious procession, walking with his servants." He seemed to believe that God, from his seat in heaven, nodded his gray locks, watching with pleasure the king of France as he walked on foot [in the service of God].

SAGNAC AND SAINT-LÉGER: LOUIS XIV'S
DOUBLE DESIGN FOR TYRANNY [2]

Voltaire named the long era from 1661 to 1715 the "Age of Louis XIV." In spite of the decline of royal power after 1688, this epoch truly deserves that name in the general history of civilization.

Louis XIV had formed little by little, without a preconceived plan, a double design which he tried to realize during the course of his reign and which he was forced to abandon . . . only by the course of events. [The first part of his design] was to reduce his subjects to absolute obedience to his commands, and the second part was to reduce Europe to complete submission. Without a doubt, as the first, most "privileged" person of his kingdom, he maintained that the privileges of the several "orders" or classes of the nation, [which he considered] underpinned his power; but if he allowed the traditional social structure to continue largely undisturbed, he nonetheless modified it in the interest of his authority, of his power, and of his glory. As he grew older, he undertook even more despotic ventures, namely that of probing into the intimate lives of private families; examining the conscience of individuals; banishing the Huguenots and stripping them of their most basic human rights; ordering demolitions and desecrations, even of the tombs of Port-Royal-des-Champs, which were razed forever; uttering the most uncivil and tactless words; and, near the close of his reign, of railing against a magistrate such as Daguesseau, or a prelate like Noailles, indeed even of disgracing a Vauban, after the services that marshal had rendered the state. Such was the tyranny which led to a general revulsion, as witness one day when an ordinary woman cried out as the King was riding by on his way to Versailles: "Whoring King." Deep down the French were never reduced to slavery. Yet it must be said that like his predecessors, and even going beyond them, Louis XIV worked with success at establishing the central government's powers in the various provinces—the oldest as well as the most newly acquired; . . . All this was preparation for the ul-

[2] From Philippe Sagnac and A. de Saint-Léger, *Louis XIV (1661–1715)*, in "Peuples et Civilisations," eds. Louis Halphen and Philippe Sagnac (Paris: Presses Universitaires de France, 1949), pp. 647–49, trans. J. C. Rule. Reprinted by permission of the publisher.

timate merging of these provinces in the eighteenth century and the Revolution, which would be, above all, the accomplishment of [a newly emerged] nation.

Nevertheless this slow and happy merger of provinces did not lead to a thoroughgoing reform of the internal administration of France, which could not be accomplished without suppressing privileges, without equality of rights as a basis for taxation, without a closely regulated financial machine, as was found in England. In France "reform from within" was always pushed to one side and more or less sacrificed to the great and glorious events unfolding outside of France.

Clearly Louis XIV wanted to dominate Europe, not so much to conquer vast reaches of territory, which would have changed the face of the world, but rather from a sense of pride and a love of prestige. He did not succeed in conquering all of the Spanish Netherlands . . . he conquered only a few provinces to the north and to the east, where the French language and traditions were already established, and [he did so] without following, anymore than had his predecessors, a preconceived plan of gaining "natural frontiers." But withal [it must be said] that he gave his realm, which in former days had been periodically invaded by the Spanish and the Germans—invasions that reached a crescendo in 1636, the year of Corbie and Saint-Jean-de-Losne, the greatest security it had enjoyed in a very long time: a security guarded by the walls of strong fortresses. *Clausa Germanis Gallia* —the Germans shut out of France—was proclaimed by a medal struck in honor of the capture of Strasbourg. Except for the momentary occupation of Lille and some associated territories in 1708 [by the Allies], Louis XIV gave France a shelter from invasion which lasted for a century and a half.

His deliberate designs, especially after 1668, for the submission of Europe to his laws, passed through many stages. At first his designs seemed to work: after Nijmegen [1679] the king, installed in the solemn and majestic setting of Versailles, appeared an Olympian god, a *Mars christianissmus* according to Leibniz's expression, or a Jupiter giving orders while holding thunderbolts in his hand. At his command the war in the North stopped and Sweden, vanquished, emerged victorious [again at Louis's command] at the treaty of Saint-Germain [1679]. Louis XIV is the arbiter of Europe: his armies, his navies, organized by Louvois and Colbert, sustained by the industrial might of the French state, are strong and ready to move, feared by all.

After this apogee of the reign comes the turning point of Louis's career, somewhere between 1682 and 1688. His destiny becomes uncertain. The "Reunions" in time of peace added to France lands extending up the Moselle to below Trier. The Revocation of the Edict of Nantes further aroused indignation, resolving Europe in its resistance to France. The Truce of Ratisbon in 1684 left Europe in precarious balance. The circle of enemies tightened; and, after the English Revolution [1688], almost all of Europe, with the Maritime Powers leading the way, rose up against the absolutism and the domination of the King of France. Outwardly Louis XIV remained still *le grand Roi,* the great king, invincible; but, in actual fact, things were already changing.

The decline of French power begins, slowly, from 1688 to 1697; thereafter it accelerated; this in spite of the radiant moment [in 1700] when Louis XIV told them: "Messieurs, here is the King of Spain," pointing to Philip V [his grandson]. However by 1708 the invasion of Flanders took place and in 1709 the king, close to complete humiliation, was saved only by the weariness of the English nation, [shaken] by the political revival and accession of the Tory party to power. Louis XIV is defeated by a coalition, which finds itself divided by a confusion of interests and a diversity of principles that separates the goals of the Maritime Powers from those of the Continent. Already French preponderance is over, at least for the moment; in fact the dismemberment of the French Empire has begun; its seapower is in decline. The balance of power shifts against France. . . .

10
Camille Picavet: The King as a Diplomatist

Camille Picavet, who taught at the University of Toulouse after the First World War, writes about the Grand Monarch without the rancor that we find in Sagnac. Using Spanheim and the Venetian ambassadors as his guides, Picavet tallies Louis's strengths and weaknesses as a diplomatist, finding that among the king's greatest assets were his unflagging love of his métier de roi, *his firmness in dealing with foreign governments and his unfailing discretion.*[1]

I. King Viewed by Foreign Diplomats

The king's good and bad qualities as a diplomatist are abundantly revealed in the writings of his contemporaries. . . . Foreigners were his most eager critics, as witness [the writings of Ezéchiel] Spanheim. "Louis XIV is not," Spanheim writes, "one of those geniuses of the first rank who sees, who penetrates, who resolves, who undertakes everything himself, who [then] formulates the plan and executes the project." This probably just means that Louis XIV was not a Richelieu. Yet [Spanheim admits] Louis knew how to make use of the ideas of his collaborators, and this collective action [of ministers and king] is so basic, so much a part of state affairs that it is nearly impossible to know actually who was the true author of such diplomatic ploys as the exploitation of the Right of Devolution [in 1667] or in the System of Reunions in peace time [1679–81].

Spanheim, however, wastes little time in getting to the heart of the matter. He notes that Louis XIV's self-conceit restricted [his understanding] of complex affairs, made him satisfied with grasp-

[1] From Camille Georges Picavet, *La Diplomatie française au temps de Louis XIV (1661–1715)* (Paris: Librairie Félix Alcan, 1930), pp. 52–53, 56–58; trans. J. C. Rule. Reprinted by permission of the Presses Universitaires de France.

ing only the superficial meaning without plumbing the depth. Spanheim adds "even if the king has enough talent to understand these great issues, he doesn't concern himself enough with them to direct them or to envisage them in all of their aspects."

[Spanheim, however] then hastens to create—by weighing positive and negative qualities—the traditional balance of a well-rounded psychological portrait. [Louis XIV, he says, showed] "a great application to affairs of state, secrecy in deliberations, a great deal of firmness in the execution of resolutions taken [in Council]. . . . [he displayed] a temperament that was naturally level-headed, one not given to being brusque, one which usually rendered him master of himself." Spanheim adds that Louis XIV spoke little and to the point. . . . Application, discretion, firmness, and composure would therefore be the essential qualities of Louis XIV as director of French diplomacy. It is these qualities which people remembered him for, which were [mirrored] in the memoirs of the time and in the letters of the French ambassadors. As to the king's faults, Spanheim enumerates them with a certain harshness: they are pride, passion for "gloire," excessive confidence in his armies, contempt for his enemies, stubbornness, and the temptation to listen to bad advice. The over-all effect [of Spanheim's appraisal] is rather confused because the king's policies are defined and judged in the same breath as his character is delineated.

Spanheim quite clearly disliked the Louis XIV of the Revocation of the Edict of Nantes and of the War of the League of Augsburg—a Louis with whom he was particularly well acquainted. [On the other hand] the reports of the Venetian ambassadors, though brief, are more laudatory: "His Majesty," relates Morosini, "possesses a particular talent for negotiations." Contarini, his successor, praises the exquisite good manners of the king, the artfulness of his replies to the ambassadors, in which, while expressing himself in an agreeable and harmonious voice, the king repeated one by one the essential points of the ambassador's speeches. . . . These are quite tangible assets [for any king]. . . .

II. Louis in Council

[Louis] presided over the High Council perhaps with less zest in the latter part of his reign than during the first years when he had just discovered his aptitude for the "métier de roi." Yet, after 1690, he presided over the Council with unflagging regularity. However [in the later years] decisions were no longer made by the majority but by the king alone, who usually spoke last. One remark made by him in 1709, which is reported by Sourches, is particularly significant. Louis XIV vigorously disapproved of the . . . Emperor Leopold I, for having followed the advice that the majority of his advisers gave him in great matters of State. In his opinion, Louis iterated, he was persuaded that a great monarch should listen to all the members of his council, but that it was up to him to weigh their advice and then choose the best.

Let's remember finally, that in order to underscore the importance of the royal role, it was Louis XIV who chose the questions to be considered by the *Conseil d'en haut*. No one had the right to question the king, or to speak about a subject that had not been submitted to the Council. Outside the Council all work was elaborated in individual conversations [between minister and king]. The most frequent and most regularly scheduled conversations were with the secretary of state for foreign affairs. This had been so from the very first years of Louis's personal reign.

For lack of other information, the correspondence which Lionne, who lived in Paris for several months during the year 1667, had with the king then in the army, furnishes us with some valuable information about their collaboration. This correspondence deals with a whole series of short and very intriguing *mémoires*; also of extracts or résumés of correspondence with ambassadors, analyses of responses made by Lionne, advice from the secretary on countless detailed affairs, and accounts of conversations with foreign ambassadors. . . . Often a letter from Lionne accompanies the documents transmitted to the king. When Lionne gave what he calls "his feeble advice" the king usually answered him. Sometimes the king was content with sending his own *mémoire* to Lionne, marked with brief marginal notes, a "no," a "good," or a short sentence, indicating the decision to take opposite each paragraph. Everything is decided by the king, even to the bonfires to be kindled at the election of the new Pope.

This double correspondence seems to be an exceptional case.

More often than not the king simply gave his orders to his secretary of state by word of mouth. . . . [As he grew older Louis tended to establish a rigid regimen; this was particularly true of his collaboration with Colbert de Torcy, minister from 1697 to 1715.] One might say that Torcy was at the king's beck and call every day. "Torcy," notes Sourches, "was accustomed always to send a messenger to see when it would be convenient for the king to speak to him." There were as many variations as there were days. The long private interviews were a rarity: the first, which took place in 1712, caused a sensation. Sometimes Torcy would arrive "a little before the end of the king's supper," waiting for the king in his cabinet, where [on the king's arrival] Torcy would read the dispatches to him for about half an hour. Sometimes [Torcy would see him] in the morning, "when the king had returned to his cabinet after mass," and when the Duke of Burgundy was present. Sometimes as one evening in 1709 [Torcy would see the king] in Madame de Maintenon's rooms, where the king . . . retired between seven and ten o'clock in the evening and worked with Chamillart, then with Torcy, the latter who carried with him the correspondence of some ambassador or other. From time to time it would happen that Torcy would interrupt the Council of Finances, where he did not sit, in order to relay to Louis XIV urgent letters. In time it became a fixed practice [for Torcy and the king] to work in the evening in Mme de Maintenon's chambers. When state affairs became pressing, the king saw Torcy twice a day—often immediately after the Council had adjourned. Every now and then other ministers were present at the session between king and foreign secretary.

III. The King in Audience

By unanimous agreement, it was said that the king excelled in his public or private audiences with foreign ambassadors. In the public audiences the king displayed his natural prudence, dignity, and reserve. His stateliness and natural "presence" served his purposes very well.

These qualities of reserve and of guardedness served the king well; but Louis XIV warned: "Too many monarchs would be quite capable of governing wisely in these matters [of foreign affairs] if they had but bothered to take time to counsel, thus being able better to prepare themselves for encounters with clever and accomplished men [such as foreign ambassadors]," and, the king warns: "on any subject under discussion a foreign ambassador can with little difficulty, at a moment's notice, and by chance or design, propose certain things which a king is not ready to discuss."

Yet however prudent he might be, Louis XIV never seemed [to observers] to be dull or colorless. At these solemn receptions he adapted himself to the circumstances and to the men. When he felt confident, when he did not fear inopportune questions, or legal dispute over etiquette—he relaxed perceptibly.

On other occasions Louis XIV, departing from his usual politeness and courtesy, raised his voice to an almost insolent pitch. [At these times] he had either made up his mind or he wished to intimidate his adversaries. This threatening manner he adopted on several occasions with the ambassadors from Holland, first with Van Beuningen, whose tone of voice upset him and against whom [he eventually] lodged a complaint with the [Dutch] States-General; he did the same with de Groot when in 1672 he had decided to go to war with the Dutch. When in 1670, Windischgraetz, envoy extraordinary from the Emperor, complained of the [French] occupation of Lorraine and requested that the matter be negotiated, following the custom of the day, with the king's commissioners, Louis XIV replied "that he himself watched over his own affairs, and rendered his own judgments. . . ."

11
Louis XIV's Gloire

With the work of Gaston Zeller (1890–1960) we clearly return to a republican tradition, but with a difference. Zeller, though generally hostile to Louis XIV, strives like Spanheim and even Saint-Simon to present a balanced portrait of the king. Taking as a touchstone Saint-Simon's Parallels between the Last Three Bourbon Kings *(or Parallel Lives of)—a more judicious work than his* Mémoires— *Zeller analyzes the attributes of kingship, particularly the concept of* gloire. *Zeller concludes his portrait by advancing the thesis that Louis probably suffered from an inferiority complex, a malady that caused the king to bluster and bully his advisers. (Compare the selection of Colbert de Torcy, Chapter 6.)*

GASTON ZELLER: GLOIRE AS MASK [1]

In order to learn more about Louis XIV as a man and as a monarch let's turn our attention to someone who knew him well: to [the Duke of] Saint-Simon.

We will begin by setting to one side some of the insidious remarks that are too often spoken of Saint-Simon by our contemporaries who in their eager attempts to glorify the great king, . . . dismiss the duke's testimony in a few lines. Take for example what Lavisse has to say: "Malicious testimony is offered [by the Duke about Louis XIV]. Some of Saint-Simon's ideas are ridiculous, some inexact, and some, even though he was by and large an honest man, seem to us today impassioned lies. This is proof enough that Saint-Simon is not to be trusted." In spite of Lavisse's warning, let Saint-Simon speak for himself; but not as Saint-Simon the author of the *Mémoires* (that endless chronicle

[1] From Gaston Zeller, *La France de Louis XIV* (Paris: Centre de Documentation, 1953), pp. 2–7; trans. J. C. Rule. Reprinted by permission of the publisher.

that portrays the last years of the reign of Louis XIV) . . . but as Saint-Simon the author of a lesser known work . . . *Parallels between the Last Three Bourbon Kings,* written in Saint-Simon's later years. . . .

Here, to begin with, is the general portrait that Saint-Simon paints of Louis XIV. It is the statesman, the monarch, who Saint-Simon attempts to capture and portray. . . . Thus we find something that is quite useful to us—no superfluous prattle about wigs, clothes, gargantuan appetites, excessive lusts for women, etc.—all the traits depicting the more than human personality of Louis XIV. Saint-Simon wants to interest his reader; and in doing so he employs a pungent style that lends itself at times to a certain clipped conciseness . . . thus as you know, his writing is often highly wrought, elliptical, and borders upon inaccuracy. But this is of less importance to us than to note that his style is usually vivid and that it admirably states what the author wishes to say.

Here is what we read from Saint-Simon; "Louis XIV was brought into the world under very fortunate circumstances. He was born good-natured, docile, patient, and with a religious faith that he retained even during the period of greatest troubles [the Frondes]. In short, he was truly a friend of justice and truth. That is he would have been if selfish flatterers had not continually caused him to sacrifice these ideals for the sake of his 'gloire' and his authority. It was this passion for 'gloire' and authority that caused him to undertake so many wars and destroy all the earlier ancient constitutional limits [of the government] that Henri IV and Louis XIII had consistently respected. Henri IV and Louis XIII deprived the nobles of their means to command fear, obedience, and tyranny. Louis XIV [went further] by utterly humbling them. To put it mildly, he overwhelmed them by any method he could contrive."

And further on Saint-Simon says: "Even with the limitations of a mediocre intelligence [he gained poise and maturity in attending the salons of his mother, Anne of Austria, of Mme de Soissons, and the salon of Mme de Montespan]." [In those salons] "Louis acquired an easy manner of speaking, always majestic, and a facility in responding in a few well chosen words to speeches of foreign ambassadors, princes, and others whom he wished to honor, or to those who brought him declarations of homage from cities and conquered territories. He seasoned these gifts with dignity. These gifts of speech and his striking stateliness of person were indeed great assets to his kingship."

Let us look at the first sentence: "His basically mediocre intelligence . . ." Saint-Simon is here a little less caustic than in his *Mémoires*, where he describes Louis XIV as being "of an intelligence less than mediocre"; there is no doubt that what we have in the *Parallel Lives* is an attempt at being a bit more objective. In the *Lives* Saint-Simon wants to play the historian; in the *Mémoires* a memorialist, which is quite a different thing. We should realize that Saint-Simon in the *Lives* weighed his words carefully when he said that Louis XIV was "of mediocre intelligence."

Let us continue our reading: Out of Louis XIV's basic conservative nature sprang his ability to control his emotions, his general distrust of people, his aversion to talent, his fear of intellectuals, and his hatred for free thinkers . . . ; on the other hand, he showed favor to those who hide their accomplishments and with whom he could thus feel at ease. . . . He often induced terror in those who approached him . . . , or a feeling of utter abasement. From Louis XIV's two great character flaws: the lack of judgment concerning affairs and people and of obstinacy arose . . . many of the great misfortunes of his reign: . . . for example, the overwhelming support he gave his Bastards [legitimated children], in making them his legal heirs, and [the immense power given his ministers] who would not have continued in office except for his support; and finally his love of petty detail, which made him feel superior to others; yet at the same time his habit of leaving the important matters of state in his ministers' hands.

More can be said of the ministers. ". . . they learned early in the reign how they could retain their positions . . . that is, by reinforcing Louis's natural mistrust and by encouraging his pride of place, while at the same time persuading him that for the sake of his dignity and of his very safety that he should trust none but them. Such was the art of the ministers from the very beginning, and such was the art of governing that was adopted by Mme de Maintenon [Saint-Simon's *bête noire*]; indeed both the ministers and Mme de Maintenon took great care to make Louis XIV believe he was not governed by them, when indeed he was. The result of all this is that his reign, for such a long time so radiant,

was so only as long as there were great ministers and generals.
. . . The decline of the reign was due to the weak successors of
those first great ministers and generals (whom the king had found
in office [in 1661]). . . . The final decline was a result of the poor
choices made by the king for the replacement [of the first generation of ministers and generals]. . . ."

We see then that this is no longer a portrait: it is a philosophy
of how one governs. I am not going to expound upon that in
detail. . . . We will say now, in any case, that Saint-Simon's
philosophy of governing is full of insight and intelligence and
consequently deserves serious consideration.

In returning to the personality of Louis XIV, if we want to
recapitulate the impressions brought out clearly in these pages
and those insights gleaned from other sources we can state that,
even though he lacked native intelligence, Louis XIV succeeded
in acquiring what we could call a polish of sorts, which impressed
those who saw him only rarely or from a distance. He knew how
to speak and for a king that seemed sufficient. This is the point
upon which the contemporaries all agree: he knew how to make
people listen and he said what had to be said.

As for having been well educated, that is another matter. His
natural talents were not extraordinary and it is untrue to say
that everything possible was done to develop them. The pam-
phleteers of the time of the Fronde, that is during the time of
Louis XIV's infancy and adolescence, said many times that his
mother, Anne of Austria, and Mazarin, an intimate friend of hers,
had intentionally kept him in ignorance so that they might hold
him in the background for as long as possible—under their yoke
as it were, so that they themselves might rule in place of the nomi-
nal king. Whether this slanderous allegation is true or not is hard
to prove. Many historians since have followed this line of reasoning, but what evidence have we? It is known who his tutors were,
but that does not necessarily mean that we are aware of the substance of what he learned or how he was taught. In any case we
must prove how long this slander, if it is that, outlived the days
of the Fronde. In fact these slanders reappear much later from
the pen of a person who had no particular cause to hold a grudge
against the memory of Louis XIV—the sister-in-law of the king,
the Duchess of Orleans, mother of the Regent, or Liselotte, as
that stout Germany lady was called by her intimate friends. . . .

Some time after Louis XIV's death, in a letter to an intimate German friend, she wrote, "It is not surprising that the late king and Monsieur [her late husband] were raised in an atmosphere of ignorance. Cardinal Mazarin wanted to reign and if he had had the two princes well educated he would not have been useful to or esteemed by them. This is what he wanted to avoid."

Saint-Simon himself also said this, perhaps a little more discreetly but with a perfect clarity on page twelve of his *Parallel Lives*. He is talking about Louis XIV's youth: "The King said with no hard feelings that he was scarcely less a prisoner of his keepers than his father had been. He was raised in the same ignorance and no one except those servants chosen by Cardinal Mazarin, who were to amuse and serve the king, went near him." And a little later, "Since then he has seemingly not thought of or complained about his education."

We can, I believe, rest assured that Louis XIV was taught very little and that having been denied by nature an exceptional intelligence he also lacked certain qualities indispensable to a [great] statesman. His weaknesses were not redressed; on the contrary they were aggravated by an excessive pride which appeared to be the dominant characteristic of his personality. He was preoccupied above all things . . . with winning the attention of his subjects, of his contemporaries, and especially of his descendants. In all of his writings Louis affirms that all of his efforts were channeled toward a unique goal: "gloire." He writes, for example, in his *Mémoires for the Instruction of the Dauphin*: " 'Gloire,' my aspiration in all things, is the principal object of my actions." In another formal text, written around 1668, addressing himself to La Petite Académie, which had just been established by Colbert in order to perpetuate the memory of the great things accomplished under his reign, he tells them, "You may judge, Messieurs, the esteem in which I hold you since I am entrusting to you the most precious thing in the world to me, my 'gloire.' "

Such expressions evidently require an explanation. Nowadays one no longer speaks this way. Perhaps it is a matter of taste but it is also a matter of vocabulary. The word "glory" is no longer used with the same frequency or meaning that it had in the seventeenth century. If one judges from the many examples taken from the literature of that time . . . it is seen that the word had a less emphatic meaning during the time of Louis XIV. In the plays of Corneille and of Racine it is not only the sovereigns but the tragic heroes and the men who are presented as having, if I may say, a certain sensitivity, who can speak, like Louis XIV, of their "gloire."

Among certain of the prose writers we find the word used in a context which may surprise us. Cardinal Retz, for example, wrote: "That which makes men truly great and raises them above the rest of the world is their love of that greatest of all mistresses, glory." This phrase "mistress . . . 'glory' " surprises us. Doubtless it is a dated expression. It warns us that we are approaching an epoch far removed from us by a seventeenth-century language and vocabulary much different from our own.

Thus without submitting to a philological study, for which we are not equipped, we strive here simply to give the word a more exact meaning. It should be translated, somehow, into modern language. We must find a less emphatic equivalent. The "glory" of our days has a very little flourish. Formerly, the statesmen of the sixteenth century spoke more modestly about their "reputation." The word "reputation" plays an important role and has a great deal of meaning. When a sovereign would say that he was thinking about his reputation everyone understood that it was the thing which was most important to him. Even in the first half of the seventeenth century Richelieu still used the word "reputation" with the same *strong* sense that it had in the sixteenth century. He recommended that kings "guard above all their 'reputation.' " "Glory" is basically the word "reputation" transposed, with a coefficient of some sort. The word "prestige" would certainly come closer to what was meant by the term "glory" in the seventeenth century. When we say that Louis XIV valued prestige it seems to me that we are fairly accurately translating into twentieth-century language this famous taste for glory that is prominent in his observations and his writings. His domestic and especially foreign policies were constantly dictated by considerations of prestige.

Saint-Simon, in a witty and learned sentence, indicates that the king's pride and his ignorance are responsible for one of the greatest mistakes of his reign: the revocation of the Edict of Nantes. "The king was becoming at that time more devout; but he was almost entirely ignorant of what was going on concerning the Edict (as he was concerning so many other things). He was desirous of increasing his glory and power and was easily taken in by a resolution which so strongly underscored these two goals. The depth of his ignorance would brook no contradiction thus accounting for the profound secrecy with which this conspiracy was conducted by Louvois, the confessor and Mme de Maintenon." Without discussing Saint-Simon's judgment point by point, we will only repeat that he detested Mme de Maintenon and that from 1683, that is to say, from the death of the queen and from the time that Mme de Maintenon was established in apartments next to the king, all the failings of the reign were attributed to her.

Louis XIV appeared to be more or less aware of his ignorance. This awareness, contrasted with his seemingly limitless pride, could well have (here we are only hypothesizing) produced in him a feeling of inferiority, or using more contemporary psychological terms, an inferiority complex. This inferiority complex can perhaps explain many things. Saint-Simon suggests it but, of course, not in exactly those words. We can verify this . . . in the *Parallel Lives*: "In shying away from men of intelligence, education, strength and insight Louis XIV turned his back on those who could have benefited him most and associated instead only with those humble admirers who either remained silent or said what he wanted to hear. This does not mean that he did not find distinguished ministers and courtiers of better character but he did not dismiss any of the former no matter how submissive and tremulous they might have been. When he failed to find a degree of comfort in them he did not hesitate to say so, and sometimes publically . . . as in the case of Colbert, Seignelay, Louvois, Barbezieux *et. al.*, . . ." And . . . on the following page, "Louis XIV, if one excludes Mme de Montespan and the pleasant surroundings of her home where the atmosphere was always exceedingly witty, feared wit even as he romped with the young courtiers in the most relaxed circumstances. He was happy with people of either sex only when he could feel superior to them or when they were clever enough to hide their wit thus making him appear superior. This is why he retained less talented ministers and why he so readily and continually gave the children of these right of *"survivances"* [2] for important positions of the Secretary of State.

In order to put this abbreviated portrait in perspective we will

[2] Right of inheritance.

observe that if the intellectual achievements of Louis XIV were modest he nevertheless worked exceedingly hard at his job. And if he committed numerous errors it was indeed not because he had not studied and labored over his notes, or had not read and reread them, or had not discussed them with his ministers. Moreover, all of the men in whom he confided, and all of the ministers to whom he turned for guidance, were, like him (I am thinking at this moment especially of Louvois and Colbert) untiring workers. He set the example and they followed it.

The case of Louis XIV proves that, for a statesman, an extreme application to his *métier* can, to a certain extent, take the place of intelligence and education.

RAGNHILD HATTON: *GLOIRE* AS UNIVERSAL CONCEPT [3]

Ragnhild Hatton (1913–   ), professor of International History at the London School of Economics, adds further amplification to the term gloire, *showing how many of the rulers of Europe—Louis's fellow monarchs—shared his desire to enhance the* gloire *of their state and the* réputation *of their princely house.*

The concern with political realities is also evident when we go beyond etiquette to Louis's conception of royal behavior in international relations. He had, like most of his fellow monarchs, a code of honor. He argued, as most of them did (exceptions can be found, one of them Augustus of Saxony-Poland), that a ruler pledged his word. Treaty obligations must not be surrendered lest trust be dissipated and allies not forthcoming; the promise and the threat must stand lest the next ones be treated lightly. But Louis, like other rulers of his time, would permit mediators to release him from his pledge. In 1678–79 a scheme was devised whereby Louis was persuaded to go back on his promise not to make peace with Leopold before the prince of Fürstenberg had been released from captivity by that prince's brother petitioning

---

[3] From "Louis XIV and His Fellow Monarchs," by R. M. Hatton, in *Louis XIV and the Craft of Kingship*, ed. John C. Rule, pp. 159–62. Copyright © 1969 by the Ohio State University Press. All rights reserved. Reprinted by permission of the author and the publisher.

Louis not to let his given word become the obstacle to a peace so eagerly desired by all Europe; similar ways were found to permit a minor concession to Brandenburg in respect of land in Swedish Pomerania, once Louis's insistence that the king of Sweden should have all his German possessions restored, as promised, had been largely effective. This loyalty to the given word was part of the *gloire,* or reputation, of the ruler, and of his *gloire* every ruler was extremely jealous. Such and such action would be against his *gloire,* Charles XII of Sweden argued; Leopold I used very similar terms; and so did William III. In twentieth-century historical writing there is too often a tendency to equate *gloire* with military glory only, or at most with military glory coupled with "magnificence." The military glory and the pomp and circumstance were obviously part of *gloire,* but it was not all of it. It is significant that when an Italian agent of Leopold's reported a conversation with Chamlay, he translated *gloire* with *Reputation* or with *Ansehen.* It is also significant that crowned heads did not reserve the term only for themselves as persons or representing the nation: Louis XIV urged Turenne to act "for the good of the state and the glory of your arms." This concept, the *bienfait* of the nation, was in Louis's case nearly always coupled with mention of his own *gloire;* and indeed, the concern for *gloire* seen in its proper perspective sprang from a preoccupation, which is discernible in most of the monarchs of the period, with the verdict of history on the individual ruler.

The very task of an absolutist ruler in respect of foreign policy (and in foreign affairs, as we have been reminded, William III acted in England as independently as any absolutist king, while in the [Dutch] Republic he had full control once he had learnt to manage the anti-Orangist regents) tended to produce certain common characteristics. The work was hard, the responsibility weighed heavily, and the reward was often gross flattery to one's face with criticism and unfavorable comment behind one's back: the latest story of favoritism, obstinacy and pride, or of stupidity, going the rounds of court and gossip. Neither William III, nor Louis XIV, nor young Charles XII drank much, fearing it might cloud brain and judgment ("I hope he does not expect good wine at my table," Louis drily commented on the arrival of an ambassador known to enjoy his glass). They read endless memoranda and dispatches, they listened to experts, and had, finally, to make up their own minds. They worried when things went wrong: Charles XII shut himself up and refused to see anyone while he got over private grief (the death of a beloved sister) and the public humiliation of the surrender of his army at Perevolochna; William burst out in a moment of despair, "There is nothing left for me here, I shall have to go to the Indies"; Louis wept over the miseries of the nation in the War of the Spanish Succession. But all three (and other monarchs of their time in other, if less drastic, dilemmas) had to grit their teeth and fight back. The very weight of their responsibility and their concern for the *gloire*, for the verdict of history upon them, helped them to mobilize reserves of personal courage. They were all determined not to leave the state entrusted to them diminished and more defenseless than when they had received it: this would be the ultimate blot on their own *gloire*. "Rather a forty years' war in the Empire," Charles XII commented on the eve of his 1718 offensive, "than a bad peace." "Shall I be the one," cried William in bitterness to Heinsius in 1701 when French troops poured into the Southern Netherlands, "to lose without a battle what I have struggled for during more than twenty-eight years?" "Never," reported Chamlay, during the Nine Years' War, "have I, in the twenty years I have known the king, seen Louis XIV so angry as when it was suggested from Vienna he should give up the gains of the Treaty of Westphalia." "What!" Louis had exclaimed, "am I to sacrifice the work of thirty years—I who have struggled so hard lest my enemies shall come into my house. . . . Rather war for ten years more."

If one is to make a distinction, and one ought to be made, between the three rulers whose attitudes have just been compared, it is between the two, William and Charles, who commanded armies in person, and Louis who, though passionately interested in the army, was no commander in his own right. A difference in degree, therefore, between William, who said, "I can always lie in the last dike," and Charles, who argued that it was up to him to risk his life encouraging the soldiers to be unafraid ("Better to die in battle than surrounded by doctors and weeping relatives," he once joked), and Louis, who, when he could not sleep because of bad news from the front, comforted himself that there was yet the grand army between the frontier and the capital. And on the personal level, in any comparison between the three, the inclination to take risks characteristic of commanders in the field, once preparations are complete, is strongly marked in William and Charles ("We must take risks while we are in luck," was one of the Swedish king's standing phrases; "his almost reckless boldness" is a recent verdict on William by a Dutch historian), and notably absent in the cautious Louis, who loved the craft of diplomacy and being at the center of things, who planned ahead for all eventualities, but who sometimes missed opportunities by being too unwilling to take risks in the military sense. Typical of Louis was also a certain doctrinaire, legalistic outlook that is particularly noticeable in his attitude to the house of Stuart after the debacle of 1688. Outward forms were insisted upon; the niceties of scrupulous use of the title "Prince of Orange" for William III was maintained for years after Louis had decided that the restoration of James II was no longer feasible, partly as a lever in peace negotiations but also, as Louis's correspondence with d'Avaux between 1694 and 1697 makes clear, out of concern for the legal position of the Stuarts. It would be offensive to a fellow monarch who had been unlucky enough to lose his crown, and against Louis's *gloire,* to expose James publicly to shame and humiliation by a premature recognition of William: if peace were not gained, such hurt had needlessly weakened James's position. And it would seem, from evidence only recently brought to light, that it was the complaint of Mary of Modena that her son would, on James's death, be just an ordinary person (*un simple*) that helped to decide Louis in favor of granting royal title to James Edward in 1701: William, it was argued, was king of England *de facto;* James II's son had the title by hereditary right, and to deny him the rank of king would be tantamount to a denial of his legitimate birth. The dangers of recognition were clearly seen, but accepted in the hope that no ill would come of it since Louis was tied by the Peace of Ryswick not to foment trouble for William in the British Isles. To break this would go against honor and *gloire;* but—it was held—if the country rose against William or, later, Anne, then armed assistance from France would be permissible. Similarly, support for a Stuart invasion in 1708 was held to be a "legitimate" retort to the allied attempts to stir up trouble for Louis in the Cévennes and to land troops in Toulon. Another field where Louis was forced into a more equivocal position than he might have preferred was the Habsburg struggle against the Turks. Louis was never the ally of the Ottomans, and in the 1660's (when his relationship with Emperor Leopold was on the whole good) he sent his contingent of 6,000 men as a member of the League of the Rhine to fight bravely in the battle of St. Gotthard, while a detachment of the French fleet joined that of Venice to do battle with the infidel at sea; but Louis took no part in Europe's defense of Vienna in 1683. The years of détente with the Austrian Habsburgs had come to an end with the fall of Lobkowitz and Leopold's renunciation of the partition treaty of 1668, and Louis felt that the most he could do to live up to the title of "His Most Christian Majesty" was to withdraw troops from his eastern frontier to make clear that he would not embarrass or hinder the fight against the Turks. The Habsburg battle against the Ottomans in the 1680's enabled the house of Austria to rally the Empire to its side, and the *gloire* that came to Leopold as the victor of 1683 was considerable. In Italy, French diplomats reported, it was Leopold's fame—not that of Louis— that rang through the land. Yet, the tradition of French policy in the Near East and Louis's own growing rivalry with Leopold over the Spanish succession prevented his playing an active role against the Turks, and his conception of his own *gloire* made it impossible for him to use the opportunity to attack Leopold.

12

Recent French Views of Louis XIV's Reign

Roland E. Mousnier (1907–   ) and Pierre Goubert (1915–   ) reflect some of the current French views of Louis XIV's reign. Mousnier has since 1958 served as director of the Center for Research on Modern European Civilization at the University of Paris, while Goubert was recently appointed assistant director of the École Normale Superieure and a professor at the University of Paris. Mousnier, drawing extensively on Louis's Mémoires, portrays a prince aware of the dangers of kingship, an innovator ready to follow the dictates of good sense and of reason of state.

ROLAND MOUSNIER: THE DANGERS OF KINGSHIP [1]

Besides the danger of being deceived, Louis XIV was faced with the danger of trying to please. . . . The following is a revealing extract from *Reflections on the 'Métier de Roi.'* Louis XIV says: "Kings are often obliged to act against their own inclinations, which may do injury to their innate good temper. They may want to please but they may often have to chastise and to disassociate themselves from men whom they naturally like." In another passage Louis says: "The errors I have made which have deeply bothered me have been because of complaisance or lack of care in listening to the advice of others. Nothing is so dangerous as weakness, no matter what form it may take. One must watch one's every inclination, and especially his spontaneous affections."

Coming from Louis this is undoubtedly a surprising confession. That Louis XIV was a good man who "enjoyed pleasing," who

[1] From Roland Mousnier, *État et Société sous François Ier et pendant le governement personnel de Louis XIV* (Paris: Centre de Documentation Universitaire, 1967), pp. 91–96; trans. J. C. Rule. Reprinted by permission of the publisher.

made his mistakes because of his desire to please, who admits them, and moreover, who regrets them—this is certainly not an aspect of his character that one usually sees. However it seems to be a credible aspect of his character. Thus the king was constantly obliged to be on guard against himself.

After the danger of being deceived, and of trying to please, the next most frequent danger is that of being thought frivolous. Louis XIV writes: "The profession of kingship is grand, noble, and delightful"—this is one of the statements which Ernest Lavisse uses to accuse Louis of taking things too lightly and of seeing only the enjoyable part of his job. But the king immediately adds a restriction: ". . . although one feels worthy of fulfilling each task to which one applies oneself, yet the king is not exempt from problems, weariness, and worries. Uncertainty leads sometimes to despair. Often there are . . . delicate situations that are difficult to untangle and one's ideas become confused."

Again there are few who think of Louis XIV as uncertain, indecisive, unable to distinguish good from bad, faced with problems and struggling with them to the point of despair: "Uncertainty leads sometimes to despair." Yet that is the situation as Louis sees it. But yet this was written not at a time—which is even more extraordinary—during the difficult wars of the second half of his reign; instead, this statement of despair comes from the year 1679, the occasion of his victory over the Allied coalition, the moment in time which is considered by historians the apogee of his *grandeur* and power. It is precisely then that he confesses his doubts, his troubles in discovering the truth, his uncertainty, and his despair.

Finally there is the perpetual danger of losing all one's prestige and influence. Every man in office is threatened with seeing himself in a moment, a second, destroyed in the esteem of those he governs. Another bit of advice: "As a fundamental rule you must never pardon those of your own rank." . . . Many men have been treated harshly, but his contemporaries first and historians second have been particularly severe with Louis.

Louis XIV: Cartesian

In order to fulfill his difficult tasks as a ruler, tasks which exposed the king to such [great] dangers, Louis XIV decided on some rules which he forced himself to follow in order to fulfill his rôle as best he could.

The first rule . . . was to follow the dictates of *reason*. From the *Mémoires of 1666* (Dreyss, I, 45) there is a passage concerning politics that is worth examining. Here are the words of Louis XIV: "And, in regard to the Dutch I want you to note that even if this enterprise had succeeded, there is no reason to conclude that they were right to engage in it, because in order to follow good counsel it is not always necessary to pay heed to the events, which, according to God's will, sometimes favor your armies and sometimes do not; above all it is necessary to make use of the mind that He has given us in order to follow reason at all times."

This passage from the *Mémoires* conforms exactly to the principles that Descartes laid down for the application of his method. Review the Third Part of the *Discourse on Method*, looking at the "moral maxims," particularly the second. With completely different vocabulary, of course, it is exactly the same principle: judge what it is reasonable to do, without flattering yourself, and in the complexity of human affairs one will invariably be right in following reason. . . . Because if one follows the reasonable course of action, one will, as Descartes says, be like the man lost in the forest: if he goes continually in the same direction, he will come out somewhere, which is much better than circling continually about the middle of the forest. Follow, then, the decision you have taken as if it were the best course possible and do not worry about the results because human interactions are so complex that the results are unforeseeable no matter what abilities one possesses. [In life] there is always an element of chance and of risk.

It is very striking to see the similarity between the thoughts expressed by Louis XIV and Descartes. It is even more remarkable, when you think about it, because Cartesianism was officially condemned by Louis XIV's regime; moreover, Cartesianism had scant support [from the clergy] since Descartes, despite his good intentions, was suspected by the Church. But it is apparent that these two lines of thought [royal and philosophical] are exactly the same and are part of a movement that accorded men of all stations a greater confidence in reason.

Moreover, it is not just reason that Louis XIV takes as a guide, it is also reason of State. Speaking of kings Louis says: "What they

[the government] seem to do contrary to the common law (meaning here natural law) is based most often on reason of State, which
by common consent is the most important law [of States], but the
least well known and the most obscure to those who do not
govern."

Thus, first there is *reason,* followed by *reason of state.* What is
reason of state? It embraces the public welfare, that is the sum
of what is necessary for the well-being, the good, and the *grandure*
of the State. It is the rôle of the king, then, to determine what is
necessary for the welfare of the State. The prince must determine
what this welfare is in the same way that he determines all his
actions: through *reason,* knowing he may be wrong but with the
will to see a course of action through once his *reason* has shown
him what path to take. And this reason of State can lead him to
violate all laws without exception, because the supreme law is
the public welfare: it is a question, then, on which hangs the life
or the destruction and dissolution of the kingdom and nation.

Another maxim of kingship is *personal* rule.

The king must govern by himself. As Louis XIV says, "the
decision requires a masterful mind," and it is not necessary to
provide justification [for your actions] since . . . the king receives special inspiration and special grace from God to carry out
his duties. Thanks to this divine aid he sees better than anyone
else what is the truth and what is best to do.

From this maxim of personal rule came Louis's declaration:

"I resolved on all matters not to have a Prime Minister. And
if you heed me, my son, you and your successors will forever
abolish that office in France because nothing rouses greater indignation than seeing the duties of kingship separated from the
title."

In this matter, it might be said that Louis XIV answered one
of the foremost demands made by the *Frondeurs.* If one reads the
pamphlets circulated during the Fronde, eight out of ten ask that
the king appoint no prime minister, especially not a foreigner,
but that he govern by himself. This desire became firmly rooted
in the hearts of Frenchmen.

However, personal government imposes upon the prince the
moral obligation of *hard work.* In the Longnon edition of Louis
XIV's *Mémoires of 1666* the following passage appears: "Two
things were absolutely necessary in my life: hard work and com-

plete freedom of choice of persons who carry out my will. It is through work that one rules, and for work that one reigns."

Thus we see how Louis envisaged the rôle of the kingship as well as the life of the king; indeed one cannot wish for a better comment on the expression: "métier de roi": that above all the king's task is that of being a dedicated workman [a man who labors diligently at his craft].

"I made it a rule to work regularly several times a day, two or three hours at a sitting with different people; that does not count the hours I spent closeted with individual ministers, nor the time I spent working at affairs that might arise unexpectedly. [There was one exception to the freedom Louis XIV allowed himself in speaking with his ministers or courtiers and that was with foreign ambassadors, "who often find in informal conversation a most favorable moment in which either to obtain or to penetrate [state secrets]; thus one must not receive these ambassadors [in audience] unless you are well prepared for the meeting."

Consequently, except for foreign ambassadors, the king allowed anyone at any time to come speak to him about state affairs; and at any time during the day the king might make decisions relating to his court; hours spent on the matters concerned with his court were quite independent of the time spent in his Council or in his study. Lionne, around 1665, explained to a distinguished foreign visitor that Louis XIV, at the time still young, worked from nine to eleven hours a day, apart from state ceremonial, which was yet another aspect of the *métier de roi.*

PIERRE GOUBERT: LOUIS XIV ASSESSED [2]

In contrast to Mousnier, Goubert dwells on Louis's contradictory nature, noting, for example, that the king's consummate skill in building alliances was often spoiled by "ill-timed displays of temper"; or that his desire to see "the Calvinist heresy" destroyed led to a diminution of his power abroad and at home; or that, isolated at Versailles, he neither saw nor cared about the emerging Enlightened ideas of the eighteenth century. Such judgments smack of Lavisse's interpretations but lack Lavisse's sureness of touch.

[2] From Pierre Goubert, *Louis XIV and Twenty Million Frenchmen* (New York: Random House, 1968), pp. 290–92, 292–94, 296–97, 314–15. Translated by Anne Carter. Reprinted by permission of the publisher.

*Goubert's contradictory vision may either be a sign of grow-
ing change or simply a reflection of our times.*

As a young man, Louis had promised himself that his own
time and posterity should ring with his exploits. If this had been
no more than a simple wish, and not an inner certainty, it might
be said to have been largely granted.

As a hot-headed young gallant, he flouted kings by his extravagant gestures and amazed them by the brilliance of his court, his
entertainments, his tournaments and his mistresses. As a new
Augustus he could claim, for a time, to have been his own Maecenas. Up to the year 1672, all Europe seems to have fallen under
the spell of his various exploits and his youthful fame spread
even as far as the "barbarians" of Asia. For seven or eight years
after that, the armies of Le Tellier and Turenne seemed almost
invincible while Colbert's youthful navy and its great admirals
won glory off the coast of Sicily. Then, when Europe had pulled
itself together, Louis still showed amazing powers of resistance
and adaptability. Even when he seemed to be ageing, slipping
into pious isolation amid his courtiers, he retained the power to
astonish with the splendours of his palace at Versailles, his opposition to the Pope and the will to make himself into a "new
Constantine," and later by allying himself with Rome to "purify"
the Catholic religion. When practically on his death bed, he could
still impress the English ambassador who came to protest at the
building of a new French port next door to the ruins of Dunkirk.

Dead, he became a kind of symbolic puppet for everyone to
take over and dress up in his chosen finery. Voltaire used him,
in the name of "his" age, as ammunition against Louis XV. On
the other side, he long stood as the type of blood-thirsty warlike
and intolerant despot. Even the nineteenth-century Bourbons preferred to celebrate their descent from "good king Henri" [IV]
with his white cockade, or from the "martyr" of 21 January.[3]
The great school of historians which flourished from 1850 until
1915[4] did not spare him, but studied his entourage and his reign
most carefully. In the twentieth century, the royalist academicians
Bertrand, with superb naïvety, and Gaxotte, with more talent

[3] Louis XVI.
[4] The school of Ernest Lavisse.

and disingenuousness, have made him a symbol of order and greatness, of Patriotism and even of Virtue. At the same time, the teaching of Lavisse which, although hostile, also shows great subtlety and unrivalled scholarship, still dominates the field in the scholarly academic tradition. Finally, there are the young historians, strongly influenced by philosophers, sociologists and certain economists, who pass over the king's personality and entourage—to be left to the purveyors of historical gossip and romance—in favour of concentrating on those problems of institutions, attitudes of mind, religious observances, social strata and the great movements of fundamental economic forces which, in their view, transcend mere individuals and events. While all this is going on, the general public is subjected to diatribes on "classicism," which is an illusion, on Versailles and its "significance," the Man in the Iron Mask, the Affair of the Poisons, on the king's mistresses, successive or contemporaneous, and on the "policy of greatness."

As absolute head of his diplomatic service and his armies, from beginning to end, he was well served while he relied on men who had been singled out by Mazarin or Richelieu but he often made a fool of himself by selecting unworthy successors. He was no great warrior. His father and his grandfather had revelled in the reek of the camp and the heady excitement of battle. His preference was always for impressive manoeuvres, parades and good safe sieges rather than the smoke of battle, and as age grew on him he retreated to desk strategy. Patient, secretive and subtle in constructing alliances, weaving intrigues and undoing coalitions, he marred all these gifts by ill-timed displays of arrogance, brutality and unprovoked aggression. In the last analysis, this born aggressor showed his greatness less in triumph than in adversity but there was never any doubt about his effect on his contemporaries whose feelings towards him were invariably violent and uncompromising. He was admired, feared, hated and secretly envied.

If, as a good libertine and a poor theologian, he began by taking little interest in the matter of religion, this became, from his fortieth year onwards, one of his favourite "personal spheres." But here he met with total lack of success. In his conflict with the great authoritarian and pro-Jansenist Pope, Innocent XI, he was forced to give way and, from a passionate Gallican became ultramontane to the point of embarrassing later popes. Against the Jansenists as a matter of policy rather than of doctrine, he only succeeded, despite repeated acts of violence, in strengthening the sect and uniting it with Gallicans in the *Parlement* and the Sorbonne and with the *richériste*[5] priests suppressed by the edict of 1695. Whatever may be claimed, the extirpation of the "Calvinist heresy" resulted in the weakening of the kingdom, the strengthening of her neighbours and a formidable amount of hatred, national and European, whether real or assumed. In the end, not many *religionnaires* were converted. They recanted, resisted, revolted or appealed to the enemy, and calmly rebuilt their churches in the Midi, while in Paris, the great Huguenot businessmen were generally tolerated because they were indispensable. The Catholic counter-reformation undoubtedly made great strides during the reign owing to the missions, the seminaries which were finally established, and the admirable Jansenist parish priests, but the basic foundations had in fact been laid long before 1661.

For some fifteen or twenty years, it was Louis's ambition to gather around his person the cream of artists and writers. In this field Colbert, who had learned his trade from Mazarin, was able to help him considerably while he had the power and the money. After 1673, money grew short and from 1689 downright scarce, while in the ill-fated year of 1694 [6] even such a magnificent undertaking as the Gobelins[7] very nearly failed. On the other hand, Louis very early began concentrating his efforts on his works at Versailles and later at Marly, and neglecting the rest. After 1680, patronage as a whole slipped away from the monarchy. Ideas became freer and more diversified and the main themes of the eighteenth century began to appear while the critical and scientific spirit progressed rapidly, shaking the old dogmatic ideas, and by that time Louis had largely lost interest in intellectual matters unless it was a case of checking some dangerous "innovation." But for fifteen years, there was a happy meeting of talents which shed, as it were, a lustre on the finest period of the reign. The young king had given proof of taste and even of daring. There was in him a very great *"honnête homme,"* in the sense of the period, capable of appreciating, singling out and

[5] *Richerism* was a form of extreme Gallicanism, or highly nationalistic defense of the rights of French liberties within the Roman Catholic Church.

[6] Year of the great famine; it is said over one million died.

[7] Royal company of tapestry makers.

making others appreciate (even Molière), and sometimes showing great tolerance. As time went on and he was burdened with other cares, less ably supported and in any case he was growing set in his ways, turning his back on changes in manners and ideas, he became obstinate or frankly gave up. The so-called *"grand siècle,"* with the "Great King" as its patron was a brilliant firework display which lasted no more than fifteen years.

A policy of greatness and prestige demanded an efficient and effective administration as well as adequate resources, both military and financial. We have followed the various endeavours undertaken in this field down the years. Now it is time to add up the reckoning.

In order to disseminate the king's commands over great distances and combat the complex host of local authorities, a network of thirty intendants had been established over the country. These were the king's men, dispatched by the king's councils and assisted by correspondents, agents and *subdélégués* who by 1715 were numerous and well organized. By this time the system was well-established and more or less accepted (even in Brittany). It met with reasonable respect and sometimes obedience. Sometimes, not always, since we only have to read the intendants' correspondence to be disabused swiftly of any illusions fostered by old-fashioned textbooks or history notes. The difficulties of communications, the traditions of provincial independence, inalienable rights and privileges and the sheer force of inertia, all died hard. Lavisse used to say this was a period of absolutism tempered by disobedience. In the depths of the country and the remote provinces, the formula might almost be reversed. Nevertheless, there is no denying that a step forward had been made and that the germ of the splendid administrative systems of Louis XV and of Napoleon was already present in the progress made between 1661 and 1715. Some of the great administrative bodies which subsequently set the tone and example for others, such as the registry office, the postal service, the highway department were even then in existence, although it must be admitted that the first of these was introduced as a purely fiscal measure, the second farmed out and the third in an embryonic state.

It is true that Louis XIV, like most men who grew up between 1640 and 1660, was incapable of rising beyond the limits of his education, let alone of taking in, at one glance, the whole of the planet on which he lived, to say nothing of infinite space. A king to the depths of his being, and a dedicated king, he had a concept of greatness which was that of his generation: military greatness, dynastic greatness, territorial greatness and political greatness which expressed itself in unity of faith, the illusion of obedience and magnificent surroundings. He left behind him an image of the monarchy, admirable in its way, but already cracking if not outworn at the time of his death. Like most men, and many kings, he had grown stiff and sclerotic with old age.

By inclination a man of taste, and a politician by nature, education and desire, he always despised those material accidents called economy and finance. Such commonplace things were merely appendages to his great plan. It never occurred to him that they could one day topple the throne of the next king but one. For him, all social upheavals and ideals were lumped together as "uprisings" and "cabals" to be forcibly suppressed.

Isolated at Versailles at an early stage by his own pride, the machinations of a woman and a few priests and courtiers, he neither knew nor cared that his age was becoming the Age of Reason, of Science and of Liberty. From first to last, he refused to recognize the power of Holland, the nature of England or the birth of an embryo German nation. He gave Colbert little support in his courageous maritime and colonial policies and failed to pursue them seriously. He was always more excited by one fortress in Flanders or the Palatinate than by all of India, Canada and Louisiana put together.

And yet he and his colleagues left behind them a France that was territorially larger, militarily better defended, with a more effective administration and to a large extent pacified. And although he neglected it and often fought against it, there was a time when he built up and maintained what was to be, for a long time to come, the real greatness and glory of France. The Age of Enlightenment was dominated, at least in part, by the language and the culture of France.

Like many another King of France, he went to his grave amid general dislike and the particular execration of Parisians. His dead body had already become a symbol. Louis was turning into the stuffed mummy singled out for future deification by the nostalgic and for supreme contempt by his passionate enemies.

All we have tried to do is to understand Louis XIV against the background of his own time without attempting to idolize him.

13
John C. Rule: Louis XIV, Roi-Bureaucrate

*In this last selection the editor looks first at the
general education of the king and then at the way in which
the impressions and ideas spawned in childhood were mir-
rored in the actions of the mature man. Finally, the thesis
both of this essay and of the book is that Louis's cautious,
judicious statecraft was admirably suited to the conditions
attendant on the emerging bureaucratic state. Seldom, in
fact, have the man and his times been better suited to one
another.*[1]

Louis XIV's Education

As the 1650's drew to a close, the court and country looked
increasingly to the young king, Louis XIV, for signs of leadership.
What manner of man was this fourteenth Louis? Would he re-
semble his timid, socially inept father, Louis XIII? Would he
take after his gregarious, hearty grandfather, Henri IV? Or would
he indeed manifest the obstinacy of his great-grandfather, Philip
II of Spain? These are questions posed not only by the generation
of the 1650's but by that of the 1970's.

It is a commonplace to assert that the Frondes provided the
young Louis with his best lessons in practical education. We
should ask, rather, what character traits in the young king were
nurtured by the Frondes, and how circumstances molded them?
The young prince had, contrary to legends current in his day, received exceptional training for his kingly role. His mother had
inculcated in him a sense of majesty of office, had deepened his

[1] "Louis XIV, Roi-Bureaucrate," by John C. Rule. Reprinted in slightly
modified form. Published originally in *Louis XIV and the Craft of Kingship*,
ed. John C. Rule, pp. 20–31, 38–43, 45–48. Copyright © 1969 by the Ohio
State University Press. All rights reserved. Reprinted by permission of the
publisher.

feeling of divine mission. Mazarin had reinforced her words by insisting that he take lessons in the political responsibilities of being king. Louis, under the cardinal's guidance, attended council meetings, heard the reading of important dispatches, and actually oversaw the writing of some diplomatic instructions. Both the regent and minister also encouraged the young king in cultural pursuits. Anne fostered an appreciation of music, religious and secular; and Mazarin introduced Louis to Italian comedy, to the opera, and to the ballet. The regent imparted to him a speaking knowledge of the Spanish language; Mazarin, of the Italian. From Louis's tutor, Hardouin de Péréfixe, Louis acquired a taste for history, particularly for accounts of his grandfather, Henri IV, who epitomized in Louis's mind the man of war, the builder of monuments—a true king, the opposite of a *roi fainéant*.[2] But above all, his mother, his principal minister, and his tutor allowed him freedom to play with his friends and his brother, Philippe, and time to indulge his childish fantasies. Play-acting may have allowed the young king to escape some of the tendencies toward morbid introspection that were so pronounced in the character of Louis XIII.

Louis, fortunately for France of the 1650's, survived his childhood diseases, including smallpox, and grew into a serious, self-possessed youth who, even at an early age, "was prudent enough to say nothing for fear of not speaking well." As he grew older, observers noted that Louis was by nature a rather passive individual, an excellent listener, a person who weighed experience and kept his own counsel. This passivity and secretiveness seem to have been born in part of fear of his father and mother. "His Royal Highness, the little Dauphin was barely three years old," Mme de Motteville noted, "when he appeared to be a source of vexation and resentment to the King [Louis XIII] who complained bitterly to the Queen . . . accusing her of encouraging his son to hate him. . . ." In later life Louis seldom spoke of his father; instead, he showed a marked preference for the memory of his grandfather Henri IV. But his conduct was governed not only by fear of his father but by resistance to the dictates of a possessive mother. Anne lavished on her sons the love that had for years found no outlet. Although Louis seems to have fought her dominance with greater tenacity and temerity than did his

[2] Do-nothing king.

brother Philippe, yet his opposition to his mother never led to an open break. In fact, they seldom openly disagreed; and when they did, it was a painful experience for them both. As a result, Louis from an early age avoided—indeed, abhorred—family quarrels and kept rigid control over his emotions. The advent of the Frondes heightened in the young king the sense of isolation and dramatized the need for secrecy. An aura of cloak and dagger pervaded the palace. Surrounded as he was by hostile and over-bearing nobles, Louis witnessed frequent confrontations between his close advisers and haughty courtiers. These quarrels impli-cated members of his own family, his overbearing cousin Condé, his supercilious and malevolent uncle Gaston d'Orleans. Even in council Louis and his chief minister Mazarin were spied upon by agents of the Fronde. These confrontations and betrayals of con-fidence served as practical lessons in statecraft. From Mazarin Louis learned the stratagems of defense: silence and secretiveness, the art of watchful waiting. It was Mazarin who in 1650 cajoled the insufferable Condé; it was Mazarin who, disregarding the snide remarks of the *Mazarinades,* had bargained with the "men of law" in 1652; it was Mazarin who had delayed his return to Paris until the right moment in 1653; it was Mazarin who gave way to Anne's insistence on a Spanish alliance in 1658. "Time and I shall conquer," wrote the cardinal. Louis's variation of this theme was "Je verrai"—"I shall see."

From this constellation of basic character traits, spawned in the nursery of his father's hate and of his mother's love, nurtured by the troubled times and reinforced by the wisdom of his principal minister, there developed a cluster of related behavior patterns and responses that dominated Louis XIV's life. They are so closely tied, so inextricably bound together, that it is hard to sepa-rate them. They include Louis's sense of politesse, of fastidious-ness, and of order; his intense dislike of disorder and of dissent; his passion for deliberation in council; his fear of betrayal; his devotion to his office; his search for *la gloire,* that is, the aggran-dizement of the state and of his reputation; his absorption in the mechanics of military campaigns, in the movement and deploy-ment of armies.

This innate sense of tidiness and order was not only character-istic of the man but of the age. The "formal French," W. L. Wiley calls them. The mechanisms of order were omnipresent: the ritual

levée, or arising of the king in the morning; his *couché,* or retirement in the evening; the ceremonies attendant on the *lit de
justice,* when the king in full regalia addressed the great judges of
his Parlement of Paris, his dukes and peers, the great officers of
the state; the formal *entrée* of an ambassador into a city or a procession of officials to the sovereign court or to the estates. Adum-
bration of such events filled hundreds of pages in the chronicles
of the day. Even in death the "formal French" could not escape
the elaborate ceremony of the state funeral. This emphasis on
order and ceremony heightened in Louis a craving for decorum
and hastened the ritualization of kingship. In this guise Louis
was a supreme classicist; and when Bossuet later spoke of the
king's greatness, it was to praise the "discipline in his armies"
and the "order in his household." Repeatedly, Racine's plays celebrate the triumph of moral and political order over the forces
and the agents of violence and rebellion. Versailles itself was a
monument to order and ritual in life. . . .

This man of order, as one can easily imagine, disliked dissent
and dissenters, whether they were ultramontanes or Jesuits, Huguenots or Quietists, aristocrats or republicans. To Louis they
were all tarred with the brush of treason, and *Frondeurs* were not
to be abided. It was the men of the Fronde that haunted his
youthful dreams. They had caused him and his family to flee from
one town to another, had frightened his mother, exiled his principal minister, emptied his treasury and questioned his authority.
Louis never forgave them, but with characteristic caution he dis-
sembled: with honeyed words he greeted his cousin Condé on his
return from Spain, and with careful attention he listened to Turenne's advice; but both men were kept under surveillance by
spies from the war office or by the army intendants. Louis's use
of the so-called surveillance system curtailed the seditious activity
of his over-mighty subjects, causing noble dissent to go far under-
ground.

A corollary to Louis's passion for secrecy and caution was his
reliance on the judgment of a few close advisers whose trust-
worthiness was well recognized. Mazarin had termed these men
"the faithful" because of their devotion to the king's cause during the terrible years of 1650–53. Louis, like Mazarin, entrusted
his government to these creatures of the crown. He protected
them, suffered their incompetence, as in the case of Louvois's son

Barbezieux, or their mediocrity, as in the cases of Michel Chamillart and Claude Le Peletier. What he could not forgive was a hint of disloyalty, and Louis kept up his guard even with his trusted servants. In council he matched them one against another, listened to their opinions, their arguments, reserving final judgment for himself. As one minister later complained, nineteen times out of twenty the king agreed with his ministers, but on the twentieth time he might override their opinion.

Caution and secretiveness, however, often led Louis into the serious fault of procrastination. It is true that some problems can lessen or disappear entirely with the passage of time. But at critical moments decisions, good or bad, have to be made. It was at these critical junctures that Louis sometimes faltered: we find him hesitant in 1672 to accept Dutch offers of peace; hesitant in 1688 to move against William III; hesitant in 1700 to accept Carlos II's will, or in 1709–10 to negotiate a peace settlement.

Yet despite all his doubts and hesitations Louis found the kingly craft to his taste: "Le métier de Roi est grand, noble, délicieux." For Louis the chief ingredient of the art of kingship seems to have been a dogged devotion to the task of "being king," an absorption in the *métier de roi*. After fifty-five years of active personal rule, Louis worked until the day of his death, hedged to the last by formalism and detachment.

By 1661, then, we may say that Louis XIV had become a "man of parts"; and it was at that moment that Mazarin chose, most appropriately, to exit from the political stage. "En France," La Rochefoucauld reflected, "tout arrive."

The Quest for Stability in Politics

Leisurely in all matters, Mazarin took a month to die. On February 9, 1661, he became too ill to carry on state business and retired to the château of Vincennes, where he died of cancer on March 9. The king, upon hearing the news, was reported to have said to his friend Grammont, "We have lost, you and I, a good friend." Yet for Louis the cardinal's death was at once a sorrow and a release. As Louis himself described the scene, he was so overwhelmed by emotion that he retired to a small chamber next to the cardinal's bedroom, where he remained in seclusion for several hours. Following his first depression, he felt an exhilaration, or, as he later expressed it, a delicious sense of freedom. When he emerged from his seclusion, he at once embarked on a course of action that he appears to have been contemplating for some time. He announced to his startled courtiers that henceforth they could address their petitions to him, that he would serve as his own first minister. Brave words. But there were many obstacles yet to overcome, the major one being Nicolas Fouquet, the superintendent of finances, who expected to be named principal minister after Mazarin died.

Fouquet was a scion of an important robe family, a brilliant, ambitious politician, and at the same time a man of incomparable taste in the arts, a modern Maecenas, in whose service were employed some of the greatest artists of the age: Le Nôtre, Le Vau, Le Brun, and Molière. As superintendent of the king's finances, he had proved himself to be a supple financier and a shrewd state banker. His position seemed unassailable. Louis, however, feared him both as a dishonest man of affairs and as a potential focus for political discontent, a symbol for future *Frondeurs*. Why, then, did he retain him in office for six months before arresting him? An explanation was later offered by Louis to his son: "Some may find it strange that I should have him serve me, when it is known that at that time his peculations were known to me . . . but I was convinced that he possessed some talents, and had a great knowledge of domestic affairs [and that] . . . he might render me essential service." Yet ultimately, Louis's fear of the spirit of the Fronde outweighed his respect for Fouquet's talents. In the months between March and September, 1661, Louis plotted Fouquet's disgrace. As the king listened to reports of the financial state of the kingdom read to him by Colbert from the register of receipts, it became apparent to both the king and his informant that Fouquet was not only withholding information about finances but might be plotting against the king himself. Colbert no doubt exaggerated the dangers, but the king was more than willing to listen. Colbert thus became Louis's instrument of liberation from what the king considered to be the threat of an over-mighty minister. As Mazarin himself had on his deathbed reportedly said to Louis: "I am acquitting myself of some of that debt [I owe] to your majesty in giving you Colbert."

On September 5, 1661, Fouquet was arrested and at once arraigned before a *chambre de justice*. This theatricality, beloved of Louis, was a splendid birthday gift to the king, who could now indeed call himself first minister.

In the following months and years Louis carefully reorganized the central government, emulating the pattern already suggested by Richelieu's and Mazarin's "narrow council." As early as March, 1661, Louis limited active participation in his council to three men: Michel Le Tellier, Hugues de Lionne, . . . , and, after September, 1661, Jean-Baptiste Colbert. These men were technically the king's ministers, and through the long reign only those men who regularly participated *en conseil* were considered of that rank. This first ministry was given the name of the "Tri-ade," the "Celestial Image of the Trinity." From time to time other members of the government were called for consultation: the chancellor, the secretary of state for the king's households, the members of the council of conscience, and, in times of grave emergency, the marshals of France; but for "everyday matters," as Condé called them, only the ministers spoke. In the 1670's the membership of the "council of three" was expanded to four, and observers, as they had in the 1640's, referred to the king's council as the *Conseil d'en haut,* or the high council. After 1690 the number of ministers increased to five, and that number remained constant until 1714, when it returned to three.

Louis selected his ministers not because of their hereditary office at court, nor because of their rank in the aristocracy, their position in the army or navy, or their eminence in the legal system; his two criteria for selection were that his advisers be dedicated to his service and that they be useful. He found these qualities most often in men of the civil service, who were not the "vile bourgeois" that Saint-Simon speaks of but members of the nobility of the pen, the administrative nobility, experts in their field who had usually long served the king in one of his larger councils or in the royal provincial administration. If these men proved not to have the probity, suppleness, and self-effacing qualities that Louis demanded, they were either relieved of most of their duties or excluded from the council altogether. . . .

Louis allowed the office of secretary of state to be purchased and held by right of inheritance, but he never permitted venality of office to infect the high council. Selection was on merit alone. Regarding conciliar matters, Louis was an iconoclast. In 1661, he excluded not only the chancellor and marshals of France but his mother, brother, princes of the blood, and, interestingly, all churchmen. In the case of the "Children of France" (the heirs apparent and presumptive), he suffered their presence, but seldom allowed them an active part in debates. Bitter complaints about the selection of ministers came from the nobility. As one courtier wrote: "The Great men of the Court, among others, M. de Turenne, were strongly dissatisfied and asked the king if he were going to give to three bourgeois the principal place in the government of the State." But Turenne's complaint made little impression on Louis. His trust was placed in "the faithful" who had served Mazarin so well and who he hoped would serve him with equal devotion. It is not that Louis altogether excluded "others"—*les autres*—from his council. When he needed the advice of experts in war or diplomacy—particularly of men like Turenne, or later, Chamlay, Tourville, or Harcourt—he would summon them to sit with his ministers. Yet, for "everyday matters" Saint-Simon was essentially correct when he later called the ministers the "Five Kings of France."

Of all the subjects that the ministers discussed, foreign affairs held the most prominent place on the agenda. Usually, the secretary of state for foreign affairs sat immediately to the left of the king and read excerpts from letters sent to him from French ambassadors and foreign ministers across Europe. Policy decisions were then debated, and the foreign secretary made notes of the replies that were to be made to the ambassadors; later, he submitted a draft of the important letters to the king (routine correspondence the secretary answered). Other major topics most often discussed in council were religious policies, reforms of the law, appointments to high office, and, during wartime, military strategy. Conciliar decisions were codified in a profusion of new ordinances, edicts, regulations of existing ordinances; of edicts in the form of declarations, commands to the secretaries of state, orders to the governors of provinces: of *lettres de cachet*,[3] usually to the intendants or to a minister; *arrêts du conseil*, that is, a type of executive order; and letters of commission to armed forces and memoirs to aid the king's executive officers. The actual letters, instructions, *arrêts*, and edicts were not drafted in council but in the bureaus of the individual ministries or by the staff

[3] Instructions in which the names and the signature were hidden.

secretaries attached to the large Council of State, privy and of parties. To expedite the flow of orders to the Council of State and to the ministries, the high council met frequently, often as many as five or six times a week. Of the scanty records we have of these council meetings those of *Mémoires of the Council of 1661*, edited in three volumes by Jean de Boislisle, are perhaps the most important. From notes of the meetings later transcribed by Boislisle we know the council met 119 days out of 179 from March to September, 1661, or on the average of twenty times a month or five times a week. The largest number of consecutive meetings was from May 2 to May 13. The council did not meet at all between August 21 and September 2 (immediately before Fouquet's arrest). At these council sessions the king was usually assisted by one of his secretaries "who held the pen," a trusted official of his cabinet who could forge his signature and who kept notes for the king's use. . . .

After the mid-1660's Louis tended to relegate routine financial and administrative matters to meetings of the council of finances and to the council of dispatches. In the latter council letters from the intendants in the provinces were discussed by the four secretaries of state, two or three ministers, and the chancellor. The council of dispatches declined in importance, however, during the latter half of the reign. By 1690 it met but twice a month and by 1714 ten times in the year. As the importance of the council of dispatches waned—and with it the influence of the council of finances—the power of the individual secretaries of state and of their bureaus increased. By 1712, for instance, the marine boasted ten bureaus, the war department, eight, and foreign affairs, eleven. These ministries contained their own archives, training schools, and hosts of agents, avowed and secret. Moreover, the marine and war departments controlled dozens of intendants who served with the armies, in the chief ports, and in the colonies. The foreign office was responsible for the direction of over forty chiefs of missions abroad. In 1715 France boasted the largest diplomatic corps in Europe, with fifteen ambassadors, fifteen envoys, and consuls in Cairo, Smyrna, Seide, and other places in the Levant. Thus in his own lifetime Louis XIV was witness to, and a moving force in, the bureaucratization of the French government. Indeed, one of his chief claims to prominence as a practitioner of the kingly craft was his willing espousal of the role of *roi-bureaucrate*.

The king's ministers divided among themselves the responsibility of corresponding with royal officials in the provinces and the municipalities. Their task was greatly facilitated by the presence in many of the provincial capitals of royal intendants, who were often chosen from among the *maîtres des requêtes* (consulting lawyers) of the Council of State.[4] Cardinal Richelieu had employed royal intendants as tax inspectors and as organizers of the war effort (after 1635) on the provincial and local level. At the time of the Fronde in 1648–49 the intendant's office was suppressed; but Mazarin, on his return to Paris in 1653, reinstated the royal provincial intendant and augmented his powers. It was not, however, until the late 1660's and the 1670's that these officials took up permanent residence in the provinces. The presence of this powerful royal official aroused a storm of protest from the provincial authorities. Jealous of their prerogatives, the municipal councilors, the syndics of the towns, the local judges and the judges of the parlements, the military governors, and many of the local nobility, singly or assembled in their estates, often challenged the authority of the "king's man," or, what was in many instances more effective, ignored his decrees. But, by the dawn of the eighteenth century, the intendants, and their assistants, the subdelegates, had become so integral a part of local administration that in many parts of France they were often regarded as allies rather than enemies. Thus one of the great accomplishments of the *roi-bureaucrate* was the establishment of the royal provincial intendant on a permanent footing.

As one critic, George Pagès, has pointed out, Louis was well suited for his task as *roi-bureaucrate*. Blessed by nature with the gift of good health, his attendance at the council was for fifty-five years unbroken. He told his son: "I made it a rule to work regularly two or three hours each sitting . . . and at any other time to whatever might rise unexpectedly." Louis built his life on a devotion to a schedule from which he seldom strayed. As Saint-Simon observed: "Naturally fond of trifles, he unceasingly occu-

[4] Council of State, Privy and of Parties. The *Conseil d'en haut*, or High Council, was the chief consultative committee of four to seven ministers. The Council of State, Privy and Parties (so called in Louis XIV's time only) was a large body of lawyers (150 or so) who heard cases of final appeal to the government (Privy) and formulated the royal laws—the edicts and arrêts.

pied himself with the most petty details of his troops, his household, his palaces, his table expenses."

The Quest for Stability in the Arts

The role of builder was in the early modern era an attribute of the kingly craft. Louis's great-grandfather Philip II of Spain, his grandfather Henri IV, and his father, Louis XIII, had all been great builders. Cardinals Richelieu and Mazarin had added to their own *gloire* by sponsoring the construction of churches, colleges, and schools. Louis was not to be outdone either by his ancestors or his ministers. From the early 1660's Louis scrutinized with childlike eagerness plans submitted to him by his architects. He was also keen to consult the Pope's architect Gianlorenzo Bernini about plans for a colonnade to be added to the Louvre, and in 1665 he sent a personal message to Bernini inviting him to Paris. Bernini replied that it would be an honor and delight "to design for a king of France, *un roi d'aujourd'hui* (a king for his times) buildings grander and more magnificent than the palaces of the emperors and the popes." The great Roman architect arrived in Paris on June 2, 1665, and departed in October, 1665, after having submitted plans for the colonnade. Although his plans were not accepted by Louis and the "Triade," the Bernini interlude is, nevertheless, noteworthy, because the Roman was a shrewd, discerning student of human nature and because he has left us one of the masterpieces of his day, a tangible sign of his visit, a bust of Louis XIV, which consciously adds to the iconography of Louis's kingship. Somehow, Bernini, who worked steadily at his portrait of Louis for three months, has made the king's features peep out from the stone in a marvelously lifelike fashion. Here are the full sensual mouth, the well-shaped upper lip, the pencil-line moustache, à la mode; and above the mouth the long, misshapen nose, the sight of which caused Louis to whisper to his brother: "Do I really look like that!" Here, too, is the arrogant tilt of the head by which Bernini tried to capture the youthful majesty of a man who for the artist and his French audience was indeed *un roi d'aujourd'hui,* the symbol of modern kingship.

For Louis the building of a colonnade at the Louvre was as much an interlude as Bernini's visit. Much to Colbert's chagrin, Louis insisted upon lavishing great sums of money on his country residences at St. Germain-en-Laye, Chambord, Vincennes, and

Versailles; the minister complained that Louis "neglected the Louvre, which is assuredly the most superb palace in the world." But the king persisted. He gave his architect Le Vau explicit commands to design at Versailles a block of buildings that would surround—literally encase—his father's old hunting lodge, which Saint-Simon called the small house of cards. Yet even as Le Vau's construction neared completion in the late 1660's, Louis was still not content. The proportion between the old and the new sections of the palace were off balance; and since Louis refused to raze the older, inner shell, new wings had to be added to round off its symmetry. When Le Vau died in 1670, he left blueprints for yet more additions to Versailles; and within six years Hardouin-Mansart, adapting Le Vau's drawings to his own specifications, began the central façade and the extension to either side of the main building of two vast wings. Behind the palace proper arose a great block of buildings that housed a *maison* of over 10,000 people. Beyond the palace grounds themselves a town sprang up, studded with *hôtels* of the great nobles and princes of the blood who made their winter home at court.

As Versailles rose, André Le Nôtre, the king's gardener, laid out around it his famed planned, or formal, garden. Aiding nature, Le Nôtre imported over 75,000 trees and had them planted in the filled-in land that stretched in front and to the sides of the palace; he also created a first and second parterre, and a Grand Canal upon which Colbert for the king's amusement and instruction floated a navy in miniature. Some 1,400 jets of water played from the fountains, and thousands of statues and urns dotted the gardens.

From every turn in the patterned floral aisles, from every glade and grotto, the attentive Le Nôtre displayed the iconography of kingship. Visitors found on all sides the legends of the kingly craft written in stone: the Apollonian image of Phoebus-Roi in the chariot of the sun gliding atop a vast pond; or Hercules-Roi, semi-concealed by an elegantly trimmed hedge, subduing the Hydra-headed image of religious non-conformity; or of Louis himself, lightly disguised as a Roman emperor, leading his victorious legions against the Teutonic hordes.

Yet beneath its façade of royal grandeur, with its iconographic and artistic splendors, Versailles appeared often as a cold, dark, damp, and malodorous pile to the courtiers who had to inhabit it. In a wickedly telling passage in his *Mémoires* Saint-Simon speaks of Versailles's seamy side:

> His apartment [Louis XIV] and that of the Queen suffer from the most dreadful inconveniences, with back-views over the privies and other dark and malodorous offices. The astonishing magnificence of the gardens is equalled only by the bad taste with which they are designed. . . . To reach the coolness of the garden's shade one is forced to cross a vast, scorching plain at the end of which there is no alternative, at any point, but to climb upwards or downwards. . . . The violence done to Nature everywhere is repellent and disgusting. The innumerable water-courses pumped or otherwise guided in from all directions make the water itself green, thick and muddy . . . and give off a vile odour. . . . From the vantage point of the gardens, one may enjoy the beauty of the whole design, but the palace itself looks as though it had suffered a conflagration in which the top stories and the roofs had been destroyed. . . . One could go on listing indefinitely the defects of this enormous and enormously costly palace and its seven more costly outhouses.

An English visitor, Lord Montague, was no more favorably impressed:

> His house at Versailles is something the foolishest in the world; he is strutting in every panel and galloping over one's head in every ceiling, and if he turns to spit he must see himself in person or his Vicegerent the Sun with *sufficit orbi*, or *nec pluribus impar*. I verily believe that there are of him statues, busts, basreliefs and pictures above two hundred in the house and gardens.

Louis, like his English visitor, seems in time to have wearied of his great palace and increasingly as he grew older sought refuge in the smaller palaces—the hermitages—that he built close to Versailles. At first he retreated to the Porcelin Trianon, completed in 1670 by Hardouin-Mansart and rebuilt in the late 1670's, with its exquisite gardens in miniature and its view of the Grand Canal. As the pleasures of the Trianon palled, Louis had the palace of Marly constructed, at the cost of 11,000,000 *livres*. The grounds contained some of the "finest gardens in the world." Even Saint-Simon admired them. "Shady avenues," he said, "changed suddenly into huge lakes, with boats and gondolas, and reconverted as suddenly into forests of impenetrable gloom, with their succession of fresh statues. . . . Such was the fate of a place which had been a den of serpents, toads, frogs, and carrion. . . ." The costs of all these magnificent piles, with their attendant gardens and water courses, was conservatively estimated at between $180,000,000 and $200,000,000.

But for Louis, Versailles was far more than another château in a long line of royal residences: it represented, above all, his administrative capital, a fact that did not escape the notice of the omniscient Saint-Simon:

> [Louis XIV's] constant residence at Versailles caused a continual coming together of officials and persons employed, which kept everything going, got through more business and gave more access to ministers and their various business in one day than would have been possible in a fortnight had the court been in Paris. The benefit to his service of the king's precision was incredible. It imposed orderliness on everybody and secured despatch and facility to his affairs.

The prime concern of the *roi-bureaucrate* had been served. He had within his sight—within the confines of one palace—his minister-servants and his courtier-clients, all of whom were petitioners for royal favors. He could say of those whom he wished to punish: "I do not know them," or, "They are people I never see," because the king was literally blind to those of whom he disapproved. Louis thus reduced the art of kingship to a timetable, which well suited his temperament, his "middling" disposition. The cadence of the kingly craft became deliberate, precise, ordered, and predictable, drained of surprises. It evolved into a ritual that could be re-enacted daily for each succeeding wave of courtiers. The king had become his own best architect of stability.

Afterword

As Louis XIV himself said of the tasks of kingship, they were at once great, noble, and delightful. Yet Louis's enjoyment of his *métier*—his craft—was tempered by political prudence. As a child he learned the lessons of circumspection. The disturbances of the Frondes caused the already introspective boy-king to build psychological and institutional barriers between himself and the outside world. At an early age he learned to listen attentively to his advisers, to speak when spoken to, to ponder evidence presented in the high council, to avoid confrontations, to dissemble, to wait. Like Mazarin he believed that time and tact would conquer. Invariably, in later years he greeted importunate petitioners with the words "I will see." In order better to assess the actions of his courtiers, the king drew not only on his own prodigious memory but on material aids: the collective recollections of his councilors, his household servants who carried tales to him overheard in the corridors, police reports, excerpts cut or copied from the gazettes, or letters intercepted by his postmasters. Yet despite all the evidence provided him by his ministers and his servants, Louis often hesitated before making a decision; he brooded, and in some instances put off decisions altogether.

As he grew older, the king tended to hide his person and his office behind a screen of Byzantine ritual. Like an icon, Louis was displayed to his troops and to his people, and like an icon he was returned for safe-keeping to his niche in Versailles, or Marly, or Fontainebleau. Even his officials seldom saw the king for more than a brief interview; many were content to be acknowledged by a regal nod of the head. And as decision-making became centralized in the hands of the ministers and their intendants, the great corporations of the realm—the municipalities, the judges, the local estates, the guilds, and at times the peasantry—contested royal encroachments on their rights and privileges. Yet to many in the kingdom, to some members of the clergy, to wealthier bourgeois, merchants, "men of the pen" (civil servants), better-to-do peasants, Louis represented a *roi d'aujourd'hui,* a modern king, an agent of stability whose struggle was their struggle and whose goal was to contain the crises of the age. To some critics of Louis XIV his reign appears as a hideous solidarity, "une sorte de monotanie passionnée." Louis XIV would no doubt have taken such a description as a compliment.

Bibliographical Note[1]

Louis XIV at once enunciates and defends his concepts of kingship in his *Mémoires*. There is no standard edition of this work, but the student who reads French will want to dip into the French-language editions, the most comprehensive of which was edited in 1806 by Philippe Grouville under the title *Oeuvres de Louis XIV*, 6 volumes (Paris, 1806); a more convenient, one-volume condensation appeared as the *Mémoires de Louis XIV*, edited by Jean Longnon (Paris, 1927). An earlier version of Longnon's work was translated into English by Herbert Wilson as *A King's Lessons in Statecraft: Louis XIV* (London, 1924). Recently Paul Sonnino has published a new translation: *Mémoires for the Instruction of the Dauphin* (New York, 1970); his edition has received a critical evaluation by H. G. Judge in the *English Historical Review* LXXXVII (1972). A valuable companion article is Paul Sonnino's "The Dating and the Authorship of Louis XIV's *Mémoires*," in *French Historical Studies* III (1964), 303–37. A sampling of Louis XIV's letters has been published by Pierre Gaxotte, ed., *Lettres de Louis XIV* (Paris, 1930). The king also left succinct but gracefully written instructions as to how best to view his palace gardens in his *Manière de montrer les jardins de Versailles*, with a preface by Raoul Girardet (Paris, 1951).

From among the vast autobiographical literature of the age of Louis XIV we can offer but a sampling. Louis's morganatic wife, Madame de Maintenon, has left many of her reminiscences in her carefully composed *Lettres*, superbly edited by Marcel Langlois, 4 volumes (Paris, 1935–39). Charlotte Elisabeth, Duchess of Orleans, Louis's indomitable sister-in-law, provides the reader with a lively, intelligent guide to Louis's court in *The Letters of Madame . . .* 2 volumes (London, 1924–25).

Among the king's chief servitors and advisers, the most prominent and the best known to posterity is Jean-Baptiste Colbert,

[1] A more extensive introduction to the bibliography of the reign is offered by the editor in *Louis XIV and the Craft of Kingship*, ed. J. C. Rule (Columbus, Ohio: Ohio State University Press, 1970), pp. 407–62.

whose papers were edited in the nineteenth century by Pierre Clément in *Lettres, instructions et mémoires de Colbert*, 10 volumes (Paris, 1861–83). His nephew Colbert de Torcy's private journal (or a part of it) was discovered and edited by Frédéric Masson under the title *Journal Inédit* (Paris, 1884). *The Letters of Louvois*, Louis's indefatigable minister of war, are sampled by Jacques Hardré (Chapel Hill, 1949).

As this present study readily attests, the Duke of Saint-Simon's works are one of the most valuable sources for the last years of Louis's reign. The best edition of the memoirs, and a monument of painstaking scholarship, is Arthur de Boislisle, ed., *Mémoires de Saint-Simon*, 43 volumes (Paris, 1879–1930). A graceful English rendering has recently been undertaken by Lucy Norton in the *Historical Memoirs of the Duc de Saint-Simon*, 2 volumes (London, 1967–68); an older, less sparkling translation can be found in Bayle St. John's *The Memoirs of Saint-Simon on the Reign of Louis XIV and the Regency*, 2 volumes (New York, 1901).

The great eighteenth-century work on the king is Jean F. M. Arouet de Voltaire, *The Age of Louis XIV*, trans. Martyn Pollack (conveniently reprinted in 1962, London). A sharply satiric view of Louis XIV by Charles Secondat, Baron de Montesquieu, is found in letters 24 and 27 of the *Persian Letters*, edited and translated by J. Robert Loy (New York, 1961).

The first three quarters of the nineteenth century give us little that is new in the way of an interpretation of the Ludovican era except for Pierre-Édouard Lemontey's insightful *Essai sur l'établissement monarchique de Louis XIV* (Paris, 1818). E. E. Dalberg, first Baron Acton, contributed a sympathetic interpretation of Louis as "the ablest man . . . born in modern times on the steps of a throne" in his *Lectures on Modern History* (London, 1906), published posthumously. The classic of nineteenth-century historiography—and perhaps twentieth-century as well—remains Ernest Lavisse's portrait of the king and his court, published in the *Histoire de France depuis les origines jusqu' à la Révolution*, Volume 7, part 2 and Volume 8, part 1 (Paris, 1908 and 1911). Brief English translations excerpted from Lemontey and Lavisse may be found in W. F. Church, ed., *The Greatness of Louis XIV: Myth or Reality?* (Second ed., Boston, 1972).

The twentieth century has witnessed a great outpouring of

works on Louis XIV and his age. Excellent introductions, which incorporate many of the latest revisions, are Ragnhild Hatton's *Europe in the Age of Louis XIV* (London, 1969) and *Louis XIV and His World* (London, 1972). Useful, particularly for its bibliographies and its cogent summaries of recent works, is Robert Mandrou, *La France aux XVIIe et XVIIIe siècles* (Nouvelle Clio series; revised edition, Paris, 1970). A more detailed and comprehensive history of the reign also by Robert Mandrou is *Louis XIV en son Temps* (Paris, 1972).

Biographies of Louis abound but there is no standard life. Pierre Goubert's *Louis XIV and Twenty Million Frenchmen* (New York, 1970) places the king and his court in economic-social context. The English translation of Goubert's work has been critically assessed by Ragnhild Hatton in the *European Studies Review* I (1970). John B. Wolf's more conventional biography, *Louis XIV* (New York, 1968), is thoughtfully reviewed by Andrew Lossky in the *Journal of Modern History* XLII (1970), 98–104. John C. Rule and contributors offer essays in reassessment in *Louis XIV and the Craft of Kingship* (Columbus, Ohio, 1970). Jacques Saint-Germain's *Louis XIV: Secret* (Paris, 1970) boasts a miscellanea of fascinating information concerning Louis's eating habits, his mania for collecting jewels, his care in planning Versailles, etc.

The vicissitudes of the king's early life are narrated by Henri Carré in *The Early Life of Louis XIV* (London, 1951); Louis's training for his *métier* is reviewed in the superb work of Georges Lacour-Gayet, *L'éducation politique de Louis XIV* (Paris, 1898 and 1923). The story of the Frondes (the series of revolts, 1648–1653) is ably retold by Ernst Kossmann in *La Fronde* (Leiden, 1954) and from the parlement's point of view by A. Lloyd Moote, *Revolt of the Judges: The Parlement of Paris and the Fronde* (Princeton, 1971). A general review of the beginning years of Louis XIV's personal reign (1661–62), with illustrative documents, is assembled by Pierre Goubert in *L'Avènement du Roi-Soleil 1661* (Paris, 1967).

The number of specialized works published on the personal reign (1661–1715) is vast.[2] Among those on international history and politics we might mention Louis André's useful survey, *Louis XIV et l'Europe* (Paris, 1950); Gaston Zeller, "French Diplomacy

[2] Emphasis here will be given to English-language works.

and Foreign Policy in Their European Setting," in F. L. Carsten, ed., *The Ascendancy of France: 1648–88*, New Cambridge Modern History, Volume V (Cambridge, England, 1961), and Andrew Lossky's thoughtful review of "International Relations . . ." in J. S. Bromley, ed., *The Rise of Great Britain and Russia 1688–1725*, New Cambridge Modern History, Volume VI (Cambridge, England, 1970). Essays on the diplomacy of the final years of the reign are included in Ragnhild M. Hatton and J. S. Bromley, eds., *William III and Louis XIV* (Liverpool, 1968).

The best introduction to the theory of absolutism, divine and profane, is still Jacques-Bénigne Bossuet's *Politique tirée des propres paroles de l'Ecriture sainte* (published posthumously in 1709) recently edited by Jacques Le Brun (Geneva, 1967). Two articles pointing up recent interpretations are: Herbert H. Rowen, "Louis XIV and Absolutism," and William F. Church, "Louis XIV and Reason of State," in *Louis XIV and the Craft of Kingship,* edited by John C. Rule (Columbus, Ohio, 1970). Less ambitious but useful is Paul W. Fox, "Louis XIV and the Theories of Absolutism and Divine Right," in *Canadian Journal of Economics and Political Science* XXVI (1960). A more specialized essay, dealing with the theory that the realm of France was the personal property of the prince, is Herbert H. Rowen's "L'Etat, c'est à moi: Louis XIV and the State," in *French Historical Studies* II (1961). The religious conflicts inherent in absolutism are discussed by W. J. Stankiewicz's *Politics and Religion in 17th Century France* (Berkeley and Los Angeles, 1960).

The practical applications of absolutist theory are explored by James E. King in *Science and Rationalism in the Government of Louis XIV, 1661–1685* (Baltimore, 1949) and by Charles W. Cole in *Colbert and a Century of French Mercantilism,* 2 volumes (New York, 1939). Reforms in the army are delineated by Louis André, *Michel Le Tellier et Louvois* (Paris, 1943). A detailed review of Louis XIV's councils is offered in the introductory chapters of Michel Antoine, *Le Conseil du Roi sous le règne de Louis XV* (Geneva, 1970). The work of Louis's police is surveyed by Jacques de Saint-Germain in *La Reynie et la police au Grand Siècle* (Paris, 1962). Growing discontent over Louis's domestic policies is detailed in Lionel Rothkrug, *Opposition to Louis XIV: The Political and Social Origins of the French Enlightenment* (Princeton, 1965) and in Eugene L. Asher, *The Resistance* to *Maritime Classes: The Survival of Feudalism in the France of Colbert* (Berkeley and Los Angeles, 1960).

The growth of Paris in the age of Louis XIV is cogently discussed by Leon Bernard in *The Emerging City: Paris in the Age of Louis XIV* (Durham, N.C., 1970). Versailles as a palace and an institution is reviewed through the eyes of contemporaries by Gillette Ziegler in *The Court of Versailles in the reign of Louis XIV* (London, 1963). Edouard Guillou's *Versailles: Le Palais du roi de Soleil* (Paris, 1963) is a brief but excellent introduction. Franklin Ford's perceptive study of Louis's nobility (the title is misleading, because the book deals also with the period before 1715) is titled *Robe and Sword: The Regrouping of the French Aristocracy after Louis XIV* (Cambridge, Mass., 1953). Roger Hahn's account of the role Louis and Colbert played in the formation of Europe's greatest scientific academy appears in *The Anatomy of a Scientific Institution. The Paris Academy of Sciences 1660–1803* (Berkeley and Los Angeles, 1971).

Louis's youthful interest in the arts is delightfully recaptured by Rudolf Wittkower in his Charlton lecture, *Bernini's Bust of Louis XIV* (London, 1951). Broader in scope and more generous of detail are Roger A. Weigert, *L'Epoque Louis XIV* (Paris, 1962), and Louis Hautecoeur, *Louis XIV, Roi Soleil* (Paris, 1953); and Bernard Teyssèdre, *L'Art au Siècle de Louis XIV* (Paris, 1967).

Index